Economic Anthropology

The Economy | Key Ideas

These short primers introduce students to the core concepts, theories and models, both new and established, heterodox and mainstream, contested and accepted, used by economists and political economists to understand and explain the workings of the economy.

Published

Austerity
John Fender

Behavioural Economics
Graham Mallard

Bounded Rationality
Graham Mallard

Cultural Economics
Christiane Hellmanzik

Degrowth
Giorgos Kallis

Economic Anthropology
James G. Carrier

Financial Inclusion
Samuel Kirwan

The Gig Economy
Alex De Ruyter and Martyn Brown

The Informal Economy
Colin C. Williams

The Living Wage
Donald Hirsch and Laura Valadez-Martinez

Marginalism
Bert Mosselmans

Productivity
Michael Haynes

The Resource Curse
S. Mansoob Murshed

Economic Anthropology

James G. Carrier

agenda
publishing

First published in 2021 by Agenda Publishing

Agenda Publishing Limited
The Core
Bath Lane
Newcastle Helix
Newcastle upon Tyne
NE4 5TF
www.agendapub.com

ISBN 978-1-78821-250-2 (hardcover)
ISBN 978-1-78821-251-9 (paperback)

British Library Cataloguing-in-Publication Data
A catalogue record for this book is available from the British Library

Typeset by Newgen Publishing UK
Printed and bound in the UK by TJ Books

Contents

Preface

This volume is intended as a brief introduction to economic anthropology for readers who are not very familiar with either anthropology or economics. This means that I have had to be selective in what I write, in a number of ways.

The most obvious way springs from the fact that economic anthropology is a large and diverse sub-part of anthropology. Its scope ranges from ceremonial exchanges on tiny islands in the Pacific through the relationship between brands and corporate value to the effects of the revaluation of the Swiss franc in 2015 on households in Poland, so that thorough coverage of all its facets is impossible. Instead, the volume is organized in terms of a small number of large processes that are repeated foci of enquiry. They are production, circulation and consumption. The justification for this is that, if people are to survive, they need to produce things; at a minimum, food, shelter and clothing. Some of these things are consumed directly by the people who produce them, but most circulate among people within a social group, and even beyond it to outsiders. At some point, however, the circulation stops, as people consume them.

My aim is to present some of the ideas that scholars have developed to help them think about aspects of those large processes. To do this I have laid out concepts and approaches in ways that focus on their essential insights as they are presented in classic texts. These often are fairly old works, but they are important because they lay the foundation for thinking about these concepts and are points of departure for the development of the field. In addition, they provide us with resources that help us to make sense of social life, whether it is what we see around us or what is in the news.

I do not, then, go into the ways that writers have elaborated and extended things such as the idea of the gift or of class or the development of mass manufacturing. Naturally, this does not do justice to the breadth of work on those concepts and approaches, but if I am successful it will give readers a basis that will help them to recognize and understand those elaborations and extensions. For those who are interested, at the end of this book I provide suggestions about what they might read to learn more of them and of the subdiscipline.

Focusing on those important concepts and approaches means that I have left out a lot of what is called ethnography, the detailed description of people's lives that is a hallmark of anthropology. That is because I do not want to cast readers adrift in a sea of detail swarming with strange terms. Instead, I have tried to present themes and ideas, with only enough descriptive material to help readers to get a sense of what those things look like in practice.

Because my main concern is economic anthropology, I am even more selective in my treatment of economics. It too is a large and diverse discipline, but the most visible part of it is neoclassical economics, which I treat as roughly equivalent to microeconomics. This has been the most prestigious part of economics since the 1970s, when it displaced Keynesian macroeconomics. Restricting attention to it is appropriate also because it closely resembles conventional, popular economic thought in many parts of the world.

So, this volume is not intended to be a survey of economic anthropology or a systematic comparison of it and the discipline of economics. Instead, it is intended to illustrate the kinds of things that economic anthropologists do, which is to say the sorts of topics that they address and the ideas that they use when they think about them, and to illustrate how these differ from what is found in much economics. What economic anthropologists do has, of course, changed over the course of time, and I illustrate the range of what they have done in the topics that I present and the examples that I use.

In addition, I have tried to make things readily understandable to those who are most likely to be reading these words, people from Western Europe and North America. I illustrate important concepts with material from many different places, as researchers have tried to apply these concepts to people in various parts of the world. A lot of my illustrations relate to Western Europe and North America, however. I have done this because illustrative material that is familiar makes it easier for readers to grasp the concepts, as well as helping to show how economic anthropology can illuminate not just large processes but also people's everyday lives.

Again, this does not do justice to the breadth of work that makes use of those concepts. Once readers can see how they apply in that familiar material, however, they will be better able to appreciate how other people can do things differently, and begin to think about how those different ways have come about and what they might mean. If this volume helps readers to do that, it will help them to understand economic anthropology and what it means to think like an economic anthropologist.

Like any piece of writing, this one reflects the author's perspective on things. Mine was shaped by the economic anthropology that I have thought about and used since late in 1978, when, with Achsah Carrier, I first did fieldwork. That was on Ponam, a small island in Manus Province, Papua New Guinea (PNG).

At that time work on economic anthropology commonly focused on what was called "villages", fairly small, local groups other than in "the West", which meant Western Europe, North America and other places dominated by liberal capitalist political-economic systems. Many of the anthropologists doing research in PNG were concerned with the effect of Western incursion on village life.

On Ponam, incursion first struck us as the juxtaposition of what looked like tradition and modernity. Islanders maintained markets with agriculturalists from the Manus mainland as they had done for as far back as anyone could remember. They used fishing techniques that harked back to the pre-colonial past and continued to make the shell money that they still used in brideprice payments. Through all of this they invoked the complex web of kinship that bound them to each other and shaped what they did. At the same time their houses, mostly rough wooden frames covered with palm leaf thatch, contained a surprising range of imported manufactured goods, and islanders asked about newsworthy events of the time, such as Soviet activities in Afghanistan and Margaret Thatcher becoming prime minister of the United Kingdom. Lurking behind all this, less visible but important, was the large number of Ponams who had migrated to urban areas of the country to work, many of them in fairly high government positions.

Trying to make sense of this juxtaposition drove us to investigate the history of Ponam and the Manus region since around 1900, when colonization first began to have an impact. The changes that turned out to be important were economic; I focused on them and Achsah Carrier focused on their social corollaries and consequences. I found myself becoming an economic anthropologist.

It turned out that economic changes in the twentieth century, and especially since the Second World War, were important for understanding how islanders fished and how they traded with those from neighbouring villages. They also were important for understanding relations between the generations and the sexes, understanding marriage preferences and patterns and understanding how people carried out ceremonial exchange.

After a bit over a year in the field in PNG and seven years teaching at the university in the capital, Port Moresby, I returned to the United States. After eight years in PNG, preceded by four years in the United Kingdom, things that I had not thought about much when I lived there 12 years before now struck me as odd. In Port Moresby our local supermarket either had bread or did not. On the other hand, I once found myself standing in an ordinary supermarket where I was living in the United States, bemused by the aisle that I was facing. It ran the whole depth of the store and both sides of it were devoted to nothing but bread, in more varieties than seemed possible. This consumerism, reinforced by lines such as "Shop till you drop" and "When the going gets tough the tough go shopping", was complemented by the growth of giving and the mixture of sentimentality and materialism that it expressed. This appeared in fabricated occasions for giving, such as Secretaries Day, but was most noticeable in Christmas shopping. That was starting earlier, was more garish and generated more criticism than I remembered. Moreover, it was in sharp contrast to PNG, where Christmas was largely absent. Even Ponam Islanders, who were Catholics, ignored it in favour of Easter.

Again, I found myself being an economic anthropologist. That was because the ideas that I had used to think about Ponam helped me to make sense of what struck me as odd in the United States. Many of those ideas were concerned with what happened when more personal and social relations of the sort that characterized life in places such as Ponam coexisted with more impersonal, market relations of the sort that characterized the encroaching Western system. Much that struck me as odd when I returned to the United States looked like a similar coexistence, of what people saw as the affectionate, familial realm in their homes and what they saw as an impersonal economic realm outside. I found this to be exhilarating intellectually, and spent a decade or so developing and extending my ideas to different areas of people's lives, thoughts and economic activities.

Ponam was a fishing village, and colleagues assumed that I was interested in coastal fishers. I ended up organizing research on fishers and others associated with the coastal waters in Jamaica – easier to get to than Papua New Guinea. People said that those waters were deteriorating and fish stocks were declining, and conservation organizations were trying to make things better. That situation could be approached in different ways, but, yet again, I approached it as an economic anthropologist.

In the two field sites that concerned me there were three sets of people interested in the coastal waters, and above them was the Jamaican government. The three sets were local people who fished inshore, those in the tourism sector and conservationists and their organizations, including a marine reserve at each site. In different ways, these three sets were concerned about the environmental health of the waters, as was the government. It became apparent, however, that they all also had a material interest in those waters.

The interest of the fishers was direct and obvious: they wanted fish to eat and sell. The tourism sector also had a direct interest, for they advertised sun, sand and sea to lure people to their hotels. Conservationists had an indirect interest that was less obvious. They wanted to maintain those reserves, and the government and EU and US aid agencies said that the reserves had to be sustainable, which meant: make money. That required having waters that would attract visitors and charging an entrance fee to them or the firms that catered to them. The government also had an indirect interest. Following structural adjustment imposed on the country in the 1980s there was a sharp decline both in the productive side of the Jamaican economy and in government revenue. Tourism was all that seemed to be left, and the government supported mass tourism as a way to boost the economy and generate money.

In the two sites, then, conservationists and the tourism sector had similar interests, and both wanted to kick local fishers out of the inshore waters. The conservationists wanted that because they were overfishing, the tourism sector said that their guests did not want them near hotel waters. Fishers were aware of this alliance, made more obvious by the fact that many conservationists had started out in or had close links to the tourism sector, and by the fact that the fishers were Black Jamaicans, while conservationists and those who ran tourist businesses were predominantly white and often incomers rather than natives.

Tourists were unlikely to see any of this. Most were there for the sun, sand and sea. Those who were interested enough to read a pamphlet about one or the other of the conservation areas or go to their websites saw pictures of a pretty fish or coral growth. These portrayed the health of the coastal waters in terms of the presence of those things and threats to that health in terms of killing fish and damaging coral. Fishers killed fish and were likely to damage coral if they anchored their boats. What the pictures did not portray was the massive growth of the two sites over the previous two or three decades, driven by growing tourism and the labour and services that it required. That labour, the tourists that it served and the buildings and beaches where they were served resulted in serious harm to the coastal environment, almost certainly more than those coastal fishers caused.

I have briefly described three projects that illustrate the pleasure of doing economic anthropology. It is a way of using the patterns of and changes in people's economic activities and relations to make sense of how they think about important aspects of their world, and of using that thinking to make sense of their activities and relations. The pages that follow will present those two kinds of making sense, and so show how asking questions like an economic anthropologist can be rewarding.

Introducing economic anthropology

To say that economic anthropology is the anthropological study of economy is true, but does not help much. One purpose of this introduction is to explain what "the anthropological study of economy" means.

The object of that study is economy, but this does not help much either, as the word has many meanings. For instance, it can mean being thrifty, as when housewives were admonished to practise economy. Equally, it can mean the interrelated activities of a social unit, such as the households in which those housewives existed and worked. When it is preceded by the definite article and becomes "the economy" it commonly means a country's economy. That can be defined in a variety of ways, but usually they revolve around making things intended to be bought and sold. For instance, commonly the health of a country's economy is taken to be its gross domestic product (GDP), effectively the total monetary value of all the finished goods and services produced in order to be sold in a given period.

Seeing the economy in terms of buying and selling may be ubiquitous, but it is fairly recent. The man often taken to be the founder of economics is Adam Smith, and the book that he wrote that laid that foundation is *The Wealth of Nations* (1976 [1776]), not *The Economy of Nations*. Wealth, prosperity and well-being were what concerned people when Smith wrote. What makes Smith and his fellows in the Scottish Enlightenment the founders of economics late in the eighteenth century is that they were some of the first in Western Europe to urge that activities related to those concerns should be guided by values different from those that guide activities in the rest of life. That is, and using our terms rather than theirs, they said that the economic and social realms of life should be kept separate. Adam Ferguson, another member of the Scottish Enlightenment, said that in the economic realm one is guided by whether activities "empty [or] fill the pocket" (in Silver

1990: 1484); in the social realm, one is guided by what Smith had earlier described in *The Theory of Moral Sentiments*.

Pointing to the vagaries of what people might mean when they talk about economy is important. Each of those different meanings indicates that there is a distinct something in the world that we might study, and, as those somethings differ, so our ways of studying them need to differ. I want to illustrate this by comparing the meanings in economic anthropology and in the predominant approach in the discipline of economics, which is microeconomics and which I treat as the foundation of neoclassical economics.

The difference between these two meanings was the focus of what is called the formalist–substantivist debate (summarized in Wilk 1996: 3–13), which occurred in the 1960s and was the last time that economists and anthropologists addressed each other directly. The debate was about the relative merits of two views of economy that Karl Polanyi (1957) called "formalist" and "substantivist". The formalist position is effectively that of microeconomics and seems to be the most common popular view of economy, probably because it is manifest every time we see an advertisement. These present what is on offer in terms of how it will satisfy one or another of our desires and how much we will have to pay for the satisfaction.

Advertisements stress implicitly the central feature of the formalist view of economy, which is a form of reasoning – one that formalists hold to be a human universal. This is what individuals do when they decide how to allocate their limited resources between the various things available to them that might help satisfy one or another of their desires. This often is stated more briefly: the allocation of scarce resources among alternative ends. This is a simple view, for its focus is the individual and that person's decision – a simplicity that makes it attractive.

A suitable image is of someone with a fixed amount of money confronting the shelves in a supermarket aisle, which suggests that this approach is concerned primarily with monetary transactions for material objects in societies with extensive market systems. This suggestion is reasonable, but thorough-going economists say that such decisions are not restricted to material objects or monetary transactions. An influential British economist of the 1920s and 1930s, Lionel Robbins, put it this way: "The distribution of time between prayer and good works has its economic aspect equally with the distribution of time between orgies and slumber" (Robbins 1945 [1932]: 26).

The alternative, substantivist position sees economy differently, not restricted to the individuals and the moment of their decision. According to Polanyi (1957: 243), it is concerned with "the means of material want satisfaction" in a society. Those means amount to the activities, relationships and systems through which objects are produced, circulate among people and, ultimately, are consumed over the course of time. These will take different forms in different societies. Polanyi identified three general forms: reciprocity, redistribution, exchange. All of them exist in every society, however in any given society and in any given realm of life one or another is likely to predominate.

Reciprocity occurs when people or groups regularly give to and receive from each other. An obvious example is when people give each other birthday presents or buy each other rounds of drinks. A less obvious one is when members of a group give and receive each other's labour, as when a set of neighbours take it in turns to get their children to school or when one member of a household does the work of shopping for food and another does the work of converting the food into a family meal. Redistribution occurs when people give things to a central figure, who then distributes them among those people, as when a government collects taxes and then distributes the money in different ways. Exchange occurs when people transact equivalents with each other, as when people buy and sell in market transactions.

Most economic anthropologists take a substantivist view, and are interested in one or another aspect of those means of material want satisfaction, although they extend this to include the satisfaction of immaterial wants as well. That leaves the question of what it means to study these things anthropologically. Such study is empirical and naturalistic.

It is empirical because it is concerned with people's thoughts and actions. In this, it shares common ground with neoclassical economics. It differs from the economics, however, in the way that it approaches them. The salient thoughts for economists are people's individual preferences at the moment when they decide how to act to allocate their limited resources, and these are simply taken as given, called "exogenous" and treated as being beyond the scope of their analytical model. For economic anthropologists, how people think about the things around them is not taken as given, but is an important topic, normally addressed by investigating the contextual, and especially social, factors that influence their thought.

For economists, the prime consequence of those thoughts is the individual's act, perhaps to purchase this bottle of wine rather than that one, or to buy neither and keep the money. Being focused on the moment of decision, economists generally lose interest in the consequences for the individual once that decision is made, although they may be interested in the consequences of a mass of such decisions – as, for instance, when they are aggregated mechanically into "market demand", which is seen to affect the price of things. Economic anthropologists, on the other hand, are interested in a range of consequences of those decisions as they play out over the course of time. They may be consequences for the individuals making that decision, for those around them and for the relationships that link them. They also may be at much larger scales, perhaps consequences for the relationship between those people and others in places far distant, such as the consequences of the English like of sweet tea and puddings in the eighteenth and nineteenth centuries for sugar plantations in the Caribbean (Mintz 1985).

To say that economic anthropology is naturalistic is to say that it is concerned with those thoughts and actions as they occur naturally in the world. This distinguishes it from economics, the most prestigious parts of which have often had a distinct air of deduction about them (see Blaug 2003; Rivzi 2003). That is, they posit that individuals have certain attributes and then deduce how they would act in different hypothetical situations. Commonly these actors are assumed to be objective maximizers, calculating how to get the greatest satisfaction of their desires for the least cost given the options available, and acting accordingly.

This is the case even with the most social-seeming form of conventional economic thought, the new institutional economics. This developed as a way to address a question that conventional economics had not answered: why individuals form groups, especially firms. It answered that question in terms of what is called transaction costs (Coase 1937; Williamson 1975). Those are different from the market price of things. Rather, they are the cost in money, time or anything else of finding out about the thing that you are thinking of buying (e.g. its quality) and the people you might deal with if you buy it (e.g. their reputation), and the cost of dealing with them (everything from credit card fees to the cost of getting to where they are located).

The argument about firms is that a person, taking into account both transaction and market costs, will calculate how much it would cost to hire others as employees who will do a variety of jobs in a firm, and also calculate how much it would cost to enter into contracts with individuals to do the different specific jobs. When it is cheaper to contract the work out, that person will do so; when it is more expensive, that person will hire employees. The result may be groups or firms, but the calculus remains individuals taken to be objective maximizers.

It is true that the growing field of behavioural economics investigates aspects of people's thoughts and actions in a more empirical and less hypothetical way, and in doing so raises questions about how objective and calculating people actually are (e.g. Tversky & Kahneman 1974). It relies in large part on experiments, however, which are not naturalistic but are artificial situations designed to highlight the variables or factors that researchers want to investigate.

Anthropology's naturalism implies a research technique that further distinguishes the discipline from economics. The most natural place to observe people's thoughts and actions and their consequences is in their daily lives in their ordinary setting, whether that be a village in sub-Saharan Africa, a chemical plant in Britain or a financial firm in the United States. The best way to learn about people in such settings is to live in the village or to work in the plant or firm for an extended period, sharing the tasks and the days of the people involved. This is participant observation, fieldwork, and, although it is not unique to anthropology, it is distinctively anthropological and a goal to which most researchers aspire. It need not be especially pertinent for those concerned with large-scale process and it is not possible for those concerned with events in the past. Even those researchers, however, usually seek to relate the economic activities that interest them to the daily lives of the people involved.

Participant observation comes with a cost and a benefit. The cost is obvious: it is hard to distinguish the effects of this or that variable, factor or process from the surrounding activities and events in people's lives, which are noise that can obscure the signal that the researcher is trying to observe. The value of experiments, one that they share with conventional surveys, is that they allow one to reduce or even eliminate that noise and so discern the effects of the pertinent factor. This was plain in a demonstration in my science class in secondary school intended to show the effect of gravity free from the noise of wind resistance. The teacher put a feather in the top of a glass tube, and we watched it fall slowly and unevenly to the bottom. The teacher then pumped the air out of the tube and turned it over, and we watched the feather drop like a stone.

Against that cost, fieldwork has important benefits that spring from the ways that it exposes us to that noise. For instance, researchers go into the field with ideas about what they want to study, but often find that the people they are studying are interested in something else, something that can become as compelling to the researcher as it is to those people. When Achsah Carrier and I started village fieldwork, we duly asked people about the things that we intended to study. They were happy to answer our questions, but then commonly asked if we had seen the ceremonial exchange that had taken place the previous week, and went on to tell us about it at some length. People are rarely the best judges of the nature of their lives, but if they find something compelling, in the way that those villagers found ceremonial exchange, there usually is a good reason for it. We found it compelling as well, and ended up using what we learned of it to understand the history and current state of the village and to address important questions in economic anthropology.

In addition, anthropologists will have a stock of disciplinary concepts that identify things that are likely to be important features of what they observe in their field sites. These concepts are like experiments, however, because they ignore the noise of people's daily lives – noise that is inescapable in the field and often is apparent to those who study historical documents. The consequences are not simple.

Exposure to the noise is a virtue, in that it can lead researchers to try to see what those concepts mean in the social lives that they are observing, meaning what is revealed not only in what people say but also in what they do, and in the relationship between the two. Attending to these is the way that researchers try to figure out, for instance, what "father" or "temporary worker" means in the field site, or what "commodity" or "household" is, how it differs from the standard academic meanings, why it does so and what we learn from that about the people being studied and about those standard concepts.

Exposure can also be a vice. This is because researchers can get wrapped up in simply trying to make sense of the lives that they confront, which one anglophone researcher likened to tuning into the middle of a soap opera in Swedish. In that, researchers can lose sight of the conceptual apparatus of the discipline, the analytical concepts and models that they need to use to shape what they learn into a form that allows them to communicate their findings with others. And, if they cannot do this, often they end up simply with tales from the field, interesting anecdotes from the intensity of fieldwork.

Recognizing both the strength and the cost of fieldwork is important for understanding what economic anthropologists say about the world. I said that immersion in the field can lead to a concern with the trees at the expense of the forest, with the minutiae of what the researcher sees in that Swedish soap opera. The result can be highly detailed descriptions that tell us nothing of substance about anything beyond the field site. This can be countered by concern with how the broader context affects what goes on in the field site.

It can be countered as well by concern with comparison and general-ization, which means with what different field sites described by different anthropologists might have in common, what broader patterns might exist and what factors might shape them. Years ago, A. R. Radcliffe-Brown (1952) said that anthropology stands on two legs, both of which have always been present in anthropology, although in different periods one or the other has been more visible. One leg is the ideographic, what he called "ethnography", the description of what the researcher observes in a particular field site. The other is the nomothetic, what he called "com-parative sociology", the development of reasonably valid generalizations about, and understandings of, social life in a range of societies. This can take two forms. One is generalizations about regions of the world where different societies seem to have aspects of social life in common, such as lowland Latin America, Melanesia, South Asia and the like. The other is generalizations about particular aspects of social life that are likely to exist in pretty much all societies, albeit in different forms, such as child-rearing, exchange, religion and the like.

In addition, those strengths and costs mean that economic anthropologists generally are unhappy with law-like generalizations of the sort that charac-terize much neoclassical economics, not to mention the physics that I was taught in secondary school. Rather, they are prone to focus on process, on how things work. That means that, if they do propose models of economic life, those are going to be probabilistic, speaking of the likelihood of different outcomes at the different stages of the process, rather than deterministic and quantifiable predictions of the final outcome.

Changing economic anthropology

Fieldwork was established as the prime disciplinary technique early in the twentieth century by Bronisław Malinowski. Commonly he is taken to have established anthropology in its modern form, and also is seen by many to have established economic anthropology. During the First World War he spent several years studying people on the island of Kiriwina, near the eastern end of what is now Papua New Guinea. He described many aspects of Kiriwina life, but is best known for his work on the *kula*. This was a practice by which people gave one another valuables as gifts, necklaces and armshells that had no apparent practical use. The result was that the *kula* formed a system of the circulation of valuables that integrated villages across the region into a fairly coherent whole. Malinowski's first book about Kiriwina, *Argonauts of the Western Pacific* (Malinowski 1922), describes and makes sense of that system.

Until the 1960s anthropology followed Malinowski in being concerned primarily with societies that existed outside the Modern West, a conventional phrase meaning societies dominated by monetary transactions in capitalist market systems. In the process, it accumulated a body of descriptions of economic life in parts of the world that were not home to most anthropologists. In the 1960s and 1970s, however, Western Europe and North America saw significant social change. This was the era of the civil rights movement in the United States, of the Events of May of 1968 in France and of women's liberation and anti-colonial agitation more generally. Combined with sharp growth in higher education in Britain and the United States, this led to reorientations in the subdiscipline and in anthropology as a whole. I want to mention some aspects of this.

One was the spread of intellectual approaches that situated the places that anthropologists study in larger political and economic systems, the sort of broader context that I mentioned previously. For instance, Achsah Carrier and I went to do research in a village on a small island in Papua New Guinea in 1979, four years after the country became independent from Australia. Many of the researchers doing work in the country were concerned with the effects of colonial capitalist incursion in village life, a topic that also interested researchers in sub-Saharan Africa and Latin America. How did people's increasing involvement with the expanding market economy affect the ways that they grew crops, hunted or fished? How did it lead to changes in the ways that they traded with those from neighbouring villages? How did it affect the ways that they interacted with fellow villagers in things such as marriage patterns, such as relations between the sexes and between those of different generations, such as ceremonial exchanges?

The most popular and far-reaching of these approaches were world-system theory, associated with Immanuel Wallerstein (e.g. 1974), and the theory of underdevelopment, associated with Andre Gunder Frank (e.g. 1966). In different ways, both argued that the societies where most anthropologists did research were shaped in important ways by their place in larger systems dominated by the capitalist, colonial and neocolonial heartland of Western Europe and North America. These approaches encouraged anthropologists to attend more closely to how their field sites were affected by their links to that heartland and to what was going on there. It also encouraged many to see those links as part of a larger system, in extreme form Wallerstein's world-system, with attributes of its own that affect the elements that are part of it and that could be an object of study in its own right.

A different sort of attention to that heartland was encouraged by decol-onization in much of Africa, where many anthropologists did fieldwork. The governments and academics of the new countries there often saw anthropologists as tokens of Western domination, and were reluctant to grant permission for research. As access to the region became increasingly difficult, anthropologists looked elsewhere, and many studied the more peripheral parts and more marginal people of their home countries and regions, which predominantly were in Europe and North America. And, once research in those places became common, anthropologists began to move away from the peripheral and the marginal and toward the central. The result, however, was not simply an attempt to portray life in this or that neighbourhood in, say, Glasgow or New Orleans. Rather, much of the work sought to address general topics through the study of people in the locality. For instance, Daniel Miller studied people in an area in north London to figure out what they were doing, and what they thought that they were doing, when they went shopping. The result was A Theory of Shopping (Miller 1998).

The increasing desire to think in terms of larger systems that extended beyond the immediate place of fieldwork occurred around the same time as another change: an increasing desire to think in terms of events that extended beyond the immediate time of fieldwork. There was growing interest in history, particularly the social and economic history of Western countries during the rise and spread of capitalist market systems. The pre-eminent work in this area is E. P. Thompson's *The Making of the English Working Class* (1968). It is concerned with the emergence of the prole-tariat in England, especially in the eighteenth and nineteenth centuries, and it attracted the interest of many economic anthropologists. This was complemented by another book that had been published earlier but now attracted renewed attention: Polanyi's *The Great Transformation* (1944). Like Thompson, Polanyi was concerned with the spread of liberal market capitalism, especially in England and especially in the nineteenth century.

As a result of these changes, economic anthropology took on important attributes that it retains at present. First, and much more so than previ-ously, researchers are concerned with societies in Europe and North America, whereas those who do fieldwork elsewhere are less likely to study villages and more likely to study towns and cities. Second, although earlier anthropologists may have debated the merits of more formalist and more substantivist approaches, by the 1980s the subdiscipline generally had abandoned formalism. Third, by 1990, and partly as a reaction to the increasing globalization of the economy, anthropologists commonly sought to relate what they observed in their field sites to broader systems and to historical changes. That interest was strengthened as the financial crisis of 2008 and the Great Recession and austerity that followed made clear the ways that the daily lives of ordinary people were linked to and shaped by changes that were going on in the financial sector, whether the bank down the street or a financial centre on the other side of the world. In pursuit of these interests, economic anthropologists do not restrict themselves to one another's writing but draw information and ideas from a number of discip-lines. Prime among these are history, sociology, geography and even some varieties of economics.

I have sketched the basic ways that scholars in the subdiscipline are prone to think about the people and processes that they confront, which is to say: what it means to study economy anthropologically. In doing so I have pointed out some of the ways that their thinking differs from the main ways that economists think about those things. As I said, the economists' way is how most people seem to think, at least when they are thinking about the economy rather than about what to put on their shopping list before they head to the supermarket, about whether they should look for a new job or about what they should get mother for her birthday. For anthropologists, these are all part of the economy.

The chapters that follow describe some of the ways that anthropologists think about the substantial economy, and the production, circulation and consumption of things, as well as some of what they have learned about them. Those descriptions will show how economic anthropology can help us to see how "economy" is not a separate realm full of disembodied maximizers governed by their own calculative reasoning, a realm guided by governments and central banks and reported in official statistics. Rather, it is what we do in the ordinary days of our lives in relations with the people around us, the things that shape that doing and the things that are consequences of it.

1

Production and what is produced

Greedy work is work that is greedy of your time. In his novel *The Firm*, John Grisham describes it when he writes of the life of Mitch McDeere, a new member of a large law firm, working 12 or 14 hours at a stretch, 16 or 18 in crunch times, when all you can do at the end of the day is have a cold dinner and maybe sleep in the office. Jack Ma, the head of Alibaba, extols it, in the form of a 9–9–6 work culture: work from nine in the morning until nine at night, six days a week. For a lot of people who work in WeWork premises, the slogan is "Don't stop when you're tired, stop when you are done". Work is where we produce things, and in greedy work it seems as if a lot is being produced. For Mitch McDeere it might be wills or contracts. For people at Alibaba it might be a functioning cloud computer. For freelance people at WeWork it might be pieces of computer code or podcasts.

Seeing work as being about the production of things and services is the conventional view. Governments and economists track the productivity of a country's workforce, the monetary value of what the average worker produces in a year; when companies try to make their workforce more productive they are trying to get their workers to produce more monetary value per person. Automation increases productivity when it replaces some workers with machines so that the same amount is produced by fewer people. Jack Ma does this simply by having the people at Alibaba work longer each day.

We recognize another way that work is about production. It is motivated, in the sense that it expresses an intent to achieve a goal, and the act of production and what is produced help to achieve it. For organizations such as Mitch McDeere's law firm and Jack Ma's Alibaba, the things produced are intended to be sold; when they are sold they generate money income, some of which goes to Mitch McDeere and Ma's employees as pay. Of course, money income is not the only reason that people work to produce things.

For instance, the people who left the cities of the East Coast to settle the American plains in the nineteenth century worked to produce a house that they could live in and a barn to hold their livestock and store their crops.

A little reflection, however, shows the limitation of this view of work and production. Yes, people work to make a product, whether wills and contracts, cloud computer systems or computer code and podcasts. Like the settler's house and barn, however, what people work to produce often is something beyond the concrete product itself. One purpose of the work, that is, is to build a successful future for the worker, however that may be defined. For those whose aspirations are less lofty, or whose position is more tenuous, work is where they produce an income for themselves to get them through another week, and they may count themselves lucky to do so, even if they have to work 9–9–6: they need food to eat, clothes to wear and a place to sleep.

This view of production focuses on the things that are produced and the people directly involved: those doing the producing and, perhaps, those who employ them. Nevertheless, it excludes a lot of the people, ideas, relationships, processes and motives that are linked to what goes on. Approaching production in the way that most economic anthropologists do, which means paying attention to production's social context, helps make these things visible.

One way to get at that approach is to take a view of production that extends beyond what is produced, the people doing the producing and the immediate intentions that motivate their activities. For one thing, the activities can be shaped by forces and factors external to them, in which case the activities will reflect those things and help make them seem self-evident, so that they become taken for granted, even if they are not what the producers intended or thought much about. A simple, imaginary example will illustrate what I mean.

A married couple with a young child living in, say, Baltimore or Liverpool have a number of demands on their time. They need to support themselves financially, keep house and look after their child, who is just starting school. If both parents are working for reasonable employers, they may be able to do all these things. If both are involved in greedy work, however, at, perhaps, a law firm and an architecture firm, they almost certainly will not.

They look at their situation, decide that something has to change and rearrange their lives accordingly. One of them loves the law and wants to stay at the greedy job and try to make it to partner in the firm. The other may decide that a future at a high-powered architecture firm is not that appealing, switch to a part-time job at a small and less demanding firm and take on the bulk of the responsibilities for their household and child. This rearrangement is a product of their work as surely as are the contracts produced by one of them and the building elevations and floor plans produced by the other. It is not, of course, something that either of them planned when they started to work or that either of them was hired to do but, rather, is an unintended consequence.

This couple are likely to see the rearrangement of their work and lives as a decision made freely by the two of them, one that reflects their individual skills and desires, their relationship and its history, their personalities and their sense of what they want. It is; but the two adults involved did not grow up in a vacuum, and they do not live in one. Rather, they were shaped by the society in which they live, which means the social arrangements, practices, beliefs and values in which they are immersed. As a consequence, their decision about rearranging things also is shaped by those factors.

That shaping does not mean that our couple blindly follow the common pattern. It does, however, increase the chance that their personal arrangement will echo it. Like many men in Baltimore and Liverpool, our imaginary husband has been brought up to value striving, achievement and the rewards that they can offer. Like many women in those places, our imaginary wife has been brought up to value as well personal relationships and caring for people. So, he stays in his job at the law firm and she moves to that part-time job. In any event, she noticed that there were few women at the top of the firm that she left, so she figured that she probably did not have much of a chance to get there.

As a consequence, their work produces something that has, on its face, nothing to do with contracts and architectural plans. That is, it produces specific gender relations, in which the male is more oriented to work outside the house and the female is more oriented to the house and work that goes on within it. In producing this in their own lives, their rearrangement helps to reproduce or recreate the social world around them, in which men strive to achieve at work while woman are more oriented to the household – a world in which women are fairly uncommon in the upper reaches of firms and professions. And in reproducing that world they make those gender positions and relations more common, to the point that they may become taken for granted and even seem natural.

I have pointed to some of the things that are not easy to see if we approach production in terms of which things of what monetary value are made, their making and the people directly involved. As I suggested, they are easier to see if we approach it in the way that economic anthropologists do, which means putting the production, or any other economic activity, and the people who do it in the relations, values and beliefs that are their larger social context. With this, we can begin to see people and their activities in terms of their relationship with other people and the things that they do and think, and begin to see what difference those relationships might make.

In the next few pages I want to show some of what this can mean in practice. I shall do so by describing aspects of the productive activities of people in three different places. Those people all need to produce in order to survive, and in technical terms the ways that they produce are likely to seem fairly straightforward. The social contexts in which they produce are different from each other, however, and from what is common in Western societies. Thus, they help to show how people in different settings can do things differently from what we might expect.

I said that I would describe people in three different places. One relates to villagers on a small island called Ponam, in Papua New Guinea. Another relates to peasant households in the uplands of Colombia. The third relates to coastal fishers in Negril, in Jamaica. Those people and places are of varying familiarity, so I describe them in varying detail. In addition, I describe them avoiding the "ethnographic present", long common in much anthropological work – the use of the present tense in ethnography, the description of the people and places of the researcher's fieldwork. Rather, I use the past tense, to avoid giving the impression that the practices and the people I describe are timeless and unchanging.

Ponam fishing

Ponam lies a short distance off the north-central coast of Manus, a large island some 270 kilometres or 170 miles to the north of the main island of New Guinea, itself just north of Australia. Ponam Island is small, only about 200 metres or 220 yards from the south shore to the north in its western part, which is where people lived when Achsah Carrier and I were there. Although the island is small, it is surrounded by a very large, shallow lagoon. Ponams spoke their own language, about as different from that of nearby people as English is from French. There were about 300 Ponams living on the island, and about 200 more were living in other parts of Papua New Guinea, overwhelmingly urban employees and their families or students (descriptions of Ponam are in Carrier & Carrier 1991; Carrier & Carrier 1989). Islanders' main productive activity was fishing, and they thought of themselves as sea people. Every household had at least two or three canoes of different sizes, wooden outriggers that could be sailed, paddled and poled. Equally, in every household someone was likely to go fishing every two or three days.

I want to describe a common form of Ponam fishing, *lawin*, and I shall approach it first conventionally, attending only to the people who are working, the tasks that they are doing and the things that they are producing. People would undertake a *lawin* expedition when a school of fish was sighted in the lagoon or when they were running short of fish. An expedition involved anywhere from 15 to 50 people on seven to ten canoes, each one of which carried a pair of wood-framed nets, each net being about 20 feet or 6 metres wide and about 12 feet or 3.6 metres high. Fishermen (and *lawin* fishers overwhelmingly were men) paddled or poled their canoes and the nets that they carried out to where the school had been sighted or to an area of the lagoon where they thought that there were likely to be a lot of fish. They would get into the water with their nets and array them in the shape of a large semi-circle, which they walked through the water to gather the fish within it. They then closed the semi-circle into a circle and collapsed its sides to form two parallel lines of nets with the fish trapped between them. They lifted the nets from the water, extracted the fish trapped in them and put them in the canoes that had carried the nets. At the end of the expedition the canoes returned to the island, each canoe's catch was divided equally among those involved with it and people took their share home.

It appears that *lawin* is a fairly simple way of producing food that is not very interesting. Broadening our view of it, however, reveals complexities. For one thing, people who wanted to produce fish could not just get canoes and nets and go. Rather, they needed the right to go, and that right depended on a person's position in the kinship system, as was the case in many other forms of Ponam fishing. In principle that meant being a descendant through the male line of the person who first had the right to bring a net on an expedition. That person usually was at least two or three generations before the current holder of the right, and the right bore that ancestor's name.

That "in principle" is important. There were four varieties of *lawin*, with seven to ten net rights in each, and not every right holder in the past had a son who had a son of his own, and so on. In other words, not every previous right holder had patrilineal descendants linking that holder to the present generation. The result was that occasionally in previous generations it was decided to pass net rights on to the descendants of daughters or to nephews, cousins or relatives who were even further afield. This meant that knowing who had the right to bring a net on an expedition required extensive knowledge of people's genealogical relationship with the ancestors whose names were borne by the different rights.

To make matters worse, there were not all that many adult men living on the island and interested in fishing using *lawin*; they had other ways to get fish and other things to do with their time. In some cases this meant that the person who exercised the right to bring a net on an expedition did not actually possess the right, but was acting with the consent of the right holder. Moreover, the limited number of interested, adult men meant that the people who paddled or poled the canoe that carried the net and who walked the net through the water were not what they ideally should have been: descendants in some way or another of the ancestor whose name was attached to the net right. Rather, crew members often were linked to the person who had exercised the net right through marriage links in the present or previous generations.

On Ponam, then, this way of producing food was carried out in terms of kinship, the births and marriages that linked those ancestors, the individual islanders who claimed to hold the net rights in the present and those they recruited to help them. Further, those claims and that recruitment made visible and important the kin relationships between people, and so reaffirmed them, just as being involved in a *lawin* expedition reaffirmed one's position in the kinship system and one's identity as a kinsman. This meant that the fish that an individual took home after the expedition were an expression of that person's identity in a web of identities in the kinship system. That production, in other words, did not just reflect the web of kin relations and identities; it also reproduced it.

In their productive activities, Ponam fishers and our imaginary married couple both reproduce aspects of the social life in which they are embedded: kinship in the case of the fishers and gender in the case of that couple. They differ, however, in important ways.

The couple saw their rearrangement of their lives and work as their own, voluntary decision, and it is unlikely that they consciously decided to conform to conventional gender expectations. There was nothing voluntary, however, in the way that Ponams saw the kinship relationships that justified people's claim to be able to bring a net on an expedition. Rather, those relationships sprang from what people saw as the objective history of who married whom and had which children. So, in no way was adhering to the consequences of that history a person's private decision. Attempting not to adhere would have produced laughter; repeated attempts would have produced outrage.

This points to another difference with our married couple. Although their decision about their lives and work may have reproduced conventional gender expectations, it is most unlikely that they saw their decision in terms of what they thought was right and proper for husbands and wives to do. On the other hand, islanders consciously espoused and obeyed, and so reproduced, that set of kin relationships and their importance in people's identities and lives.

It is true that people in Europe and North America can enact and reproduce kinship and other social ties and identities in their productive work. David Halle (1984) describes this among those who worked in a chemical plant in the United States that he calls Imperium. He says that, of 121 blue-collar workers, 37 per cent were close relatives: "[T]here are twenty-three brothers and seven brothers-in-law. Ten men are cousins, twelve fathers or sons, and six uncles or nephews" (Halle 1984: 5). For the people he describes, then, kin relations and identities can be important for shaping people's participation in production. For Halle's workers, however, and unlike Ponams and their fishing, kinship confers no right to produce, for that arises elsewhere. Rather, links between close kin were the route through which information passed: information about a vacancy at the plant and the nature of the work, as well as information to the boss about the nature of the relative who would be applying for the job (this is described in Grieco 1987; an early, influential analysis is Granovetter 1973).

In technical terms, Ponam fishing is pretty simple. Viewed more anthropologically, however, it illuminates the nature of social relations and identities in Ponam society and how they affect people's productive activities and are reproduced by them. This illumination in turn encourages us to ask if there is something similar in more familiar settings, such as Halle's workers at Imperium. Similarity is there, but not identity, and the differences point to how different sorts of social relations can influence productive activity in different ways in different social systems.

Colombian peasants

Peasant production in upland Colombia is described in Stephen Gudeman and Alberto Rivera's *Conversations in Colombia* (1991). Agriculturalists in the eastern Andes worked land that ranges from relatively fertile fields at lower altitudes to fairly barren areas higher up. Whatever the altitude, their staple crop was potatoes. In addition, they were likely to own some forest land that they used for firewood, as well as livestock: cows for their milk and meat, oxen for ploughing. As with Ponam fishing, the technical aspects of their productive activities were fairly straightforward and likely to be familiar to people in the West, even if they know about them only from watching movies. Those peasants planted and harvested potatoes, tended livestock and cut trees. Like Ponam, however, the social context and organization of these peasants' activities differs from what Westerners are likely to know about.

Their agricultural production revolved around the kin relationships and identities of a family: husbands and wives, parents and children, brothers and sisters. This means that the productive unit and the right to participate in it were more voluntary for Colombian peasants than for Ponams. The productive Colombian household was based on the voluntary marriage of the husband and wife who were its heads; children could, and did, leave the household, either to set up households of their own or to migrate elsewhere. In contrast, the productive Ponam *lawin* expedition was based on the allocation of net rights among dead ancestors and the descent history that linked them to living Ponams, and islanders could not deny or abandon these links.

Different productive tasks were allocated to different members of the household, and what was produced was part of the pool of household resources, used to reproduce the household and, if possible, to improve its position. This reflects the fact that, even though the senior active male was the head of the household, people saw the holding as belonging to, and the responsibility of, the household as a unit.

In *The Great Transformation* Polanyi (1944) called this way of organizing production "householding". English serfs, American settlers on the frontier and Prussian peasants commonly organized their productive activities in this way. More than that, it is a model of production that goes back to ancient Greece, for it is the *oikos* of Aristotle, a unit that, ideally, was self-sufficient, producing all that it consumed.

The *oikos* and the household of the serf and settler were not, of course, wholly self-sufficient, and neither were the upland households that Gudeman and Rivera describe. They all needed at least some things that they could not produce. Aristotle's *oikos* may have traded with neighbours for things that it needed, but the others were likely to buy them. The way that those Colombian peasants thought about that need and satisfying it are what make these households worth special attention.

The Colombian peasants produced things with two immediate ends in view. One was consumption by household members that would sustain them through the agricultural cycle and so reproduce them and their relationships, and thus the household itself. The other was sale for money in nearby markets, that money mostly being used to purchase the salt, oil, nails and other things that the household consumed but did not produce. The existence of these two ends indicates, then, that the sack of potatoes or container of milk that they produced had two different values. One of these is realized when the milk or potato is consumed: the way that it satisfies hunger and nourishes a person. That is called its use value. The other is the value that is realized when it is sold in the market: the money that household members get in exchange for it. That is called its exchange value. In producing both use and exchange value, these householders were involved in two economic realms: the household and the market.

The reproduction and prosperity of the household were their central concerns, and they drew a clear conceptual distinction between it and the market. The household was the productive unit on which they relied and with which they identified, and they saw it as the source of their lives and livelihood. The resources that the household contained included the people within it who did the work, the land associated with it, the livestock that grazed on that land, the tools and equipment that people used in their agricultural and related activities, the seed stock stored for planting in the next agricultural cycle and the agricultural produce that was surplus to what the household needed to consume to get itself through to the next harvest.

Together, these resources were seen as the household base, and people were anxious not to diminish it but, instead, to maintain or increase it. They did so through practising thrift, ensuring that as little as possible of what the household produced was consumed or sold, so that as much as possible could be devoted to securing and extending the base. Their thrift, then, was different from that of the miser, who hoards things simply in order to possess them. Instead, these households sought to retain things in order to use them productively to secure and extend their base.

I said that households produced things that had both use value and exchange value. In this they were like Ponams and their fishing, for what islanders caught could be food for the family or be taken to a local market and sold for cash or traded for a variety of foodstuffs. It is not just Ponams and Colombians who produce things that have both use and exchange value. Pretty much everyone everywhere who produces does so. Colombian peasant and Ponam fishers differ from most people in societies with extensive production and market systems, however – because the potatoes and the fish have use value for the peasants who grow them and the fishers who catch them.

In this, they differ from the steel boxes produced by a factory worker in Lyon, the contract drawn up by Mitch McDeere and the computer code written by someone in a WeWork shop. Those things all are presumed to have a use value for somebody. If they did not, it would be assumed that no one would buy them and so no one would bother to make them. They have no noticeable use value for the people who make them, however; they are produced to satisfy market demand and not personal need. Their use value is, instead, realized only by those who purchase them and consume or use them. From the perspective of those who make them, then, they are produced for their exchange value. This makes them commodities. That term has a variety of meanings, as will become clear in the chapters that follow. A central one, however, is things that are produced with the intention of selling them in a market transaction.

The Ponam and the peasant may produce things that end up being sold. Until the size of the catch or the crop can be balanced against the needs of the household, however, it is not clear whether the fish in this net or the potatoes in that sack will be consumed or sold. Consequently, those fish and potatoes cannot be said to be produced in order to sell them in the way of those steel boxes, contracts and code. They are not, then, commodities.

Jamaican fishermen

The inshore artisanal fishermen based on the fishing beach at Negril fished primarily with traps, which they called pots, that were baited with sweet potato and placed on the bottom of the sea fairly close to the shore. They also trolled with hook and line, but only when they were travelling in their motor canoes from the fishing beach to their pots and back again. They checked their pots regularly. If there were fish in them they would lift the pot, extract the fish, renew the bait and put the pot back on the sea bottom. They sold their catch to small, local shops and restaurants (most of the fish served in tourist restaurants was frozen and came from Central America).

Like Ponam fishing, then, the technical side of this trap fishing is simple. I describe it here because the social side differed from that of both Ponams and Colombians. In Negril, fishers spent a lot of time on the beach, keeping their pots and canoes in good repair and socializing with each other. They were not a community, however, in the way that Ponam fishers and Colombian householders were. Rather, as Andrew Garner, a researcher who did fieldwork there, put it, the fishing beach was the place where 40 or 50 independent businessmen carried out their activities. They may have known each other for years and some may have been kin to each other, but this had no noticeable effect on who did what or on their dealings with each other in their fishing.

Their productive activities, then, did not reflect and recreate their relationships with each other and the identities and obligations that can arise from them. Rather, they reflected and recreated fishermen's independence, which they asserted strongly when they talked about the coastal waters and their fishing. This independence did not arise from some state of nature, however. Rather, it was a creature of the colonial history of Jamaica, and of the Caribbean more generally.

The important aspect of that history is the importation of large numbers of Black African slaves, primarily to work on the plantations that were central to the economy of islands throughout the region well into the twentieth century. Those slaves existed alongside a much smaller number of White settlers. Some of them were plantation owners or managers; some were merchants, shippers and the like; some were specialists, such as shipwrights and mechanics, or professionals, such as accountants, clerks and lawyers. This meant that race and economic activity were closely related – and they have remained so into the present.

Historically there was no significant commercial fishing in the region, and the salt fish that remains a valued foodstuff there was imported from far to the north. There was small-scale, inshore fishing, however, of the sort that took place in Negril. Male slaves carried out this fishing, primarily to produce food for the plantations that owned them. With their owners' consent, however, they took the opportunity to fish on their own account, selling their personal catch in local markets where slaves traded. Historically, then, there was an association between small-scale fishing and relative freedom from oppressive constraint, an association that continues to affect the way that many people in the region think about fishing and the coastal waters (Price 1966).

Another factor complemented this cultural link between Black men, fishing and autonomy. Concerned White settlers, some of them ministers of religion or colonial officials, repeatedly sought to improve what they saw as the undesirable condition and behaviour of the local Black population. These White settlers mostly saw Black women as agents of change and were focused on schools and churches, institutions that seemed suited to instil the order and self-discipline that local Black men especially were seen to lack. A common result, certainly not what those concerned White people intended, was the association of Church and school, Whites, women and constraint.

This became manifest in a cultural opposition between what Peter Wilson (1973) calls respectability and reputation. The former was seen as relatively female, pious, hierarchical and conformist. It was also seen as fairly White and colonial, because of the people who encouraged it, and relatively town-based, because of the location of those schools and churches. The latter was seen as relatively male, egalitarian, autonomous and disruptive, occasionally called "slackness" by people I talked with, which meant lacking the respect and decorum valued by the middle-class Jamaicans who used the term. In addition, it was seen as fairly Black and anti-colonial, and located mostly on the beaches, which were neither town nor plantation areas.

When those Negril fishermen were socializing on the beach and in its small restaurants and rum shops, and when they were independently carrying out their productive activities, they were reflecting and recreating a set of associations that were based on the region's history and that remained important in people's understandings of their world, of themselves and of their place in that world.

I have described some of the productive activities of sets of people in Papua New Guinea, Colombia and Jamaica to illustrate what we can learn if we approach economic activities anthropologically.

One way that I did so was by seeing the people doing the producing as more than so many units of labour power or as expending so many hours of time in work. The units and hours may be important for those measuring a country's economy, but they ignore what interests economic anthropologists. This is because they do not see those people as anything more than those units and hours, a view as impoverished as that of the neoclassical economist who sees the person shopping for a child's birthday party as nothing more than a given set of unexplained, exogenous preferences and a limited amount of money. And the sets of people that I have described illustrate important elements that the impoverished view misses.

One simple thing that it misses is how people think about what they are doing, which shapes how they do it. This is especially clear with the Negril fishers. They were not simply producing fish, for they were also being independent and egalitarian, which had no technical basis and may even have reduced the amount that they caught. And the values that they placed on those attributes not only reflected the history of the region, but also set the beach off from town, men off from women and reputation off from respectability.

Another thing that the impoverished view misses is apparent in what I said of Ponam fishing and Colombian peasant agriculture. That is the way that relations between people that have their origins outside the realm of production can shape who produces with whom, and can do so in different ways. For Ponams, the relationships were pretty much given at birth, for they were the facts of kinship and descent. For the Colombians, they were the more voluntary and transient relationships of the household. I said that relationships can be important for modern-day industrial workers, but in a different way. They are channels through which information passes rather than a basis of the right to produce, as on Ponam, or the organization of the productive unit, as in Colombia. That is because the authority to organize or carry out that production rests not with those workers but with the people who employ them.

Economic anthropologists have long studied how social relations are linked to production, and thus far I have illustrated that study in terms of how things were in the place and time of research. Things have doubtless changed on Ponam, at Negril and in the Colombian uplands. Such change does not, however, erase the fact that those fishers and peasants illustrate some of the ways that people can carry out production and some of the factors that shape the way that they do things.

The examples that I presented in this chapter look at how production works at a given time, and I have used that to address different aspects of the relationship between production and its social context. In what follows I pursue the topic in terms of processes and events as they unfold over an extended period of time. Doing this allows us to begin to see how a change in one of them can affect the other, and so understand better the relationship between production and context.

2

Changing production

The previous chapter introduced and illustrated the sorts of things that concern economic anthropologists studying production, which take into account social relations and cultural values that are ignored by the common economistic view. I now continue the exploration of that economic-anthropology approach, moving away from the fairly small-scale and static focus of the preceding pages. Instead, I attend more to larger-scale, dynamic processes, while still being concerned with how they are linked to people's ordinary lives, relationships and understandings.

Those processes are the historical changes in production in Western Europe and North America. In the Preface I said that one reason for focusing on those regions is that they are likely to be familiar to most readers, so that it will be relatively easy for readers to make sense of what I write. There is another reason, however. That is to make the familiar seem strange. That means helping readers to see how the familiar things in their world are not to be taken for granted. One way to do that is to show how familiar things could be different – and, indeed, have been different. With any luck, the history described in this chapter will help to do that.

Although it is less dominant than it was in the 1970s and 1980s, mass production using the moving assembly line remains an important image of production. The development of this sort of production is commonly presented in terms of the engineers who designed new ways of making things and the technical developments that made those designs possible. The engineers and technical developments were there, and were necessary. Focusing on them, however, ignores what interests economic anthropologists: the changing relationships among producers and between producers and what they make.

I want to describe the historical development of mass production, sketching changes that began in Britain in the sixteenth century, led to the Industrial Revolution and continue into the present. An important part of this process was the appearance of industrial capitalism, and its political-economic aspects are well-trodden ground. That appearance and those aspects are described in detail by analysts inspired by the work of Karl Marx (e.g. Braverman 1974), the core of whose view is laid out in Part I of *The Communist Manifesto* (Marx & Engels 1948 [1848]). The social and cultural aspects that I describe are less familiar.

I present them by sketching a set of steps taken in many countries that shifted from agriculture to industry, although I focus on how they occurred in England and the United States. The first of these is cottage industry. That is followed by what is called "putting out", which is a form of contracting production out. Then comes early factory production and, finally, modern factory production. As will become apparent, these mark a continuing change in the organization of production that reflects the changing interests of those doing the organizing, and I consider how those interests have changed since the flourishing of modern factory production. That change meant that producers' relationship with their work changed. It also seems to have involved a significant change in what at least some influential people think that production is for – a change that has had a range of effects on the society, culture and politics of the countries involved.

Cottage industry

In cottage industry, the household uses its own equipment, labour and social relations to produce things intended for sale. A classic description of the cottage production of cloth in England is by Neil Smelser (1959), which I draw on here (see Carrier 1992). Except for the fact that cottage industry involved the production of things intended to be sold, it resembles the Colombian peasants already described.

In terms of the issues of concern here, an important feature of cottage industry is that the production process occurred in household space and reflected household organization. Typically, the father, the head of the household and the person who directed production, owned the loom used in weaving, while his wife was responsible for spinning the yarn that her husband wove. In the process, the father taught his sons weaving and the mother taught her daughters spinning and the subsidiary operations involved in cloth production. Once the cloth was finished, it was sold to a merchant or at a market.

Householders not only used their own tools, equipment and raw materials when they produced, they also controlled the timing of production, so that it reflected their needs and interests. Such households commonly ran farms as well, and produced cloth during agricultural slack times. In other words, their weaving was only one of a set of activities in which they produced what they needed to survive. Certainly, they had to weave cloth for sale if they were to get all the things that they needed and wanted. Nevertheless, they were less dependent on regular commodity production and market transactions than were, say, people who worked as clerks in London at the time, who could survive only because they were paid a regular wage that they could use to buy what they needed.

As I noted, production relations reflected household relations, so that the cloth that household members produced also reflected them. This means that the cloth was linked to them as a possession. I shall explain this concept briefly here, as I return to it later on. A possession is something that bears the identity of the person or people who possess it, and it is different from property, which marks only legal ownership. To say that something is a possession is not to say that the possessor likes it. Rather, it is to say only that the possessor and the possession are linked in a personal way, each a part of the identity of the other. I have baked bread that ended up more suited to be used as a doorstop than to be eaten, but when I threw the loaves out they were still my bread. Making something is not the only way that it becomes a possession, and, as will become apparent later in this chapter, not everything that people make is their possession.

In cottage industry, members of the household cooperated with each other in production because of necessity. The son who assisted his father in weaving knew that the household had to produce if it were to prosper, or perhaps even survive. In addition, however, and like those Colombian peasants, their cooperation reflected their social bonds to each other, which emerged from the shared work of production as well as from their normal living and interacting with each other. So, that son was bound to his father in enduring, personal ways, as his father was to him. The son may have loved his father, but the bonds existed whether the son loved him, liked him, resented him or hated him.

The heyday of cottage industry is long gone, but the combination of economic activity and household social relations persists. It does so in attenuated form, however, because children are much less likely to be involved and because such households now are much more likely to rely primarily on commodity production for their survival than they are to use such production to complement their other economic activities.

For instance, small shops often are family affairs even if the business legally is an independent entity. In the classic small bakery the husband works in the back doing the baking and the wife works behind the counter dealing with customers. Like the cloth of the weaving household, the baked goods that they produce are their possession, reflecting in important ways their relations, actions and skills and shaping in important ways who they are. Unlike the weaving household, however, they need to bake and sell their wares regularly, which means that they are more constrained in the timing of their productive activities, less able to pace them in a way that reflects their own interests and relations.

The people who run that small bakery are members of what is called the petit bourgeoisie. They are of the bourgeoisie because they are capitalist, owning the tools and equipment used in the production of commodities. They are petit because they are a small business and rely heavily on their own labour rather than on employees. Many of those who provide services of different sorts are petit bourgeois. The man I see regularly to make my back better uses his own skilled labour and equipment and owns his premises, where his wife works in another room as a marriage counsellor. In different ways, the same sort of mix of the familial and the economic exists with the lawyer whose spouse is the office secretary, with the woman who oversees the cleaning of the stairs in the building where I live and whose mother does much of the work, and with the electricians, builders and plumbers who have "Tom Wilson & Sons" painted on the side of the company van.

To extend a point made earlier, these examples of the petit bourgeoisie show one advantage of looking at cottage industry. Being in the past, cottage industry seems alien, which leads us to see it as a distinctive way of organizing economic activity. Puzzling out that distinctiveness, however, makes it possible to think about the economic activity that we see around us in new ways. Looking at the alien past in this way is like looking at alien societies in long-term fieldwork. Making intellectual sense of the alien can help to make the strange seem familiar, and that can give us a more distanced perspective on the familiar world around us and so see it in new ways.

Putting out

The putting out system emerged in cloth production in England late in the seventeenth century, although it had appeared among craft producers in London in the middle of the sixteenth. Technically it was, effectively, the same as cottage industry, especially in its early stages. Many of its other aspects, however, were not. That is because, in putting out, the weaver entered into an agreement with a merchant capitalist, which specified the size and quality of the cloth to be produced, as well as the date when it was to be finished, collected and inspected, and the weaver paid. In its early form the merchant would advance the necessary yarn to the weaver; later the merchant might provide yarn already fixed to the weaving frame, or perhaps even a complete loom.

This arrangement meant that the weaving household abandoned control of aspects of the production, so that the resulting cloth was less a reflection of the needs and desires of the producers and more a reflection of the needs and desires of the merchant capitalist. Consequently, the cloth was more separated from the producers than it was under cottage industry, which is to say that it was more alienated from them.

Most obviously, once they contracted with a merchant, weavers lost control of the timing of production and of the nature and quality of what was produced. Additionally, the more that the merchant provided them, such as yarn, the fewer of their skills they employed, such as spinning, and the less of what they used to produce was their own. Equally, with putting out weavers were no longer able to influence the social and market relations with those who consumed the cloth, who were invisible to them. This loss of aspects of control by weavers reflected what putting-out merchants desired: a supply of finished cloth of a predictable quantity and quality at a predictable time, so that they could sell the quantity and quality of cloth that their own customers desired.

Like cottage industry, some features of putting out exist in the present, though, again, with less involvement of children. It has been fairly common in the making of clothing and shoes (e.g. Pennington & Westover 1989), and with the spread of the internet it exists in other areas of work. Computer coders or copy-editors who work via the web are likely to work from home, although they are likely to do all the work on their own, so that the social relationships that existed between producers in cottage industry have disappeared. Working at home, they own the space of production, which is likely to be household space, as well as the tools and equipment involved. Like those putting-out weavers, they have little control over the timing of production. Unlike them, however, and like the small bakers, they need regularly to transact the commodities that are the product of their labour.

The emergence of putting out illustrates again what we miss if we focus on the technical aspects of production and the commercial value of the product. The technical operation of weaving did not change with the appearance of putting out. I have shown how other aspects of production changed, however, and did so in ways that made the finished cloth less of a possession, a reflection of the weaving household, its skills, desires and relations, and more a commodity, something produced to satisfy the desires of others in return for money.

Early factory production

The most obvious change that occurred with the appearance of early factory production was that production moved out of the producers' households and to a central place. Further, that place was under the control of the capitalist factory owner rather than under the control of the producer in the way that it had been in cottage industry and putting out. In addition, production decreasingly took place in household relations and increasingly took place instead in what are called commodity relations. I need to explain what this means.

For Colombian peasants, as for those in cottage industry and putting out, the people involved in production were linked to, and constrained by, each other in social relations that reflected their fundamental and durable identities, such as father or mother, son or daughter – the sort of identities that also defined which Ponam had the right to bring a net on a *lawin* expedition. In commodity relations, on the other hand, people are linked in less durable and personal ways, and if they are workers they are linked only through their employment (see Barnett & Silverman 1979). In that, people sell to an employer their labour power, their ability to work, for a specific length of time in return for pay. When the work shift is over, workers and employers are independent of each other and can walk away. The situation is very different for those Colombian peasants and English weavers. After the potatoes had been harvested and the cloth completed, those who did the producing still were husband and wife, parents and children, brothers and sisters to each other.

This shift to impersonal commodity relations in production did not happen all at once, but took place gradually with the spread of early factory production. I want to sketch how this shift proceeded.

Much early factory production did not use commodity labour in the conventional sense but, instead, used something like the contracts for production of putting out (see Staples 1987). The person who contracted with the factory owner engaged his or her own assistants to help with the production – assistants who commonly were close relatives. Thus, production took place in terms of an impersonal commodity relationship between factory owner and contractor and a more personal, familial relationship between contractor and assistants.

Although early factory production saw the continuation of familial relations, albeit in attenuated form, it led to other things that weakened the association between producers and what they made. For one thing, factory owners could see productive activity more readily than could the merchants who put work out to weaving households, and they could use that to change production practices so that they would better suit their interests.

Perhaps more importantly, factory owners were better able than household producers to make use of the new machinery that was appearing at the time. This meant that producers were no longer using their own tools and equipment. Further, it led to a fragmentation of production, because producers increasingly made only a part of the object produced rather than the whole of it, in the way that a weaving household produced a whole cloth. Moreover, those who produced did so increasingly as minders of the new machinery rather than as the skilled workers they had been previously. For those who did the work, then, production decreasingly was the efforts of skilled artisans who used their knowledge to shape the making of things – things that were an expression of the producers. Instead, increasingly it was a process organized by owners and implemented by workers who often did little more than tend a machine that was owned by someone else and that carried out only a part of the production process, and did so in a space that was not theirs. Workers, then, were less and less likely to be seen as producers, in the way that the putting-out capitalist saw the weaver's household members as people who make cloth. Instead, increasingly they were seen as a factor of production that was to be used as efficiently as possible.

This is apparent in the way that supervision and mechanization came together in a cultural shift, as described by E. P. Thompson (1967) – a change in the nature and place of time in production and in society more generally. Thompson says that under older systems of production time was fluid, because often it was defined by the task at hand and its rhythms, and by the other demands on the time of those doing the producing – a fluid view that was part of the general culture. With the combination of increased mechanization and supervision this changed. The increased fragmentation of production that came with mechanization meant that factory owners wanted to ensure the coordination of different tasks, and they installed clocks in their factories to instil that coordination and used their increased supervision to enforce it. Decreasingly, then, was time a reflection of the work carried out by skilled producers who controlled the pace of work. Rather, it became an external reality imposed on workers that governed their work, as it came to be seen more commonly as the frame in which people lived their lives.

Modern factory production

As modern factory production gradually emerged, it weakened both the ability of workers to affect the nature of production and the social relations between workers that had existed under early factory production. As a result, workers were increasingly alienated from each other, the process of production and its products. They were, then, less and less the makers of things and more and more appendages of a production process that they did not control. This is most apparent in manufacturing, in which things were made from interchangeable parts on an assembly line.

In this system, the control of production and the regulation of work activities no longer come from contractors recruiting close kin to work for them. That is because in modern factories workers are hired as individual sources of labour power by the firm, although, as I have noted, kin links could remain important for passing on information about jobs. Moreover, that control no longer comes from owners or supervisors overseeing workers to ensure that they do what they are supposed to do when they are supposed to do it. Rather, the source of regulation is the design of the plant in which workers perform their tasks and the equipment that they use, which reflect the interests of the owners rather than the workers.

An extreme form of this is plants owned by the Ford Motor Company, especially the one at Highland Park, near Detroit, built in 1910 (see Hounshell 1984: ch. 6). In older forms of mass production, the different sorts of operations called for in producing something were carried out in separate departments in the plant. So, if a piece being produced required milling, it was taken to the milling department. This meant that the plant was organized at least partially in terms of spaces devoted to different sorts of operations and staffed by different sets of workers with their different skills and tools. Highland Park, however, was designed in a way that reflected more purely and relentlessly the production process. For instance, as an automobile front axle was being produced it moved through the plant on a specified path. If, at a particular point on that path, the axle needed milling, a milling machine was placed there. The old departments, then, disappeared, and so did their sets of workers with their shared skills, tasks and interests.

The plant and its equipment also reduced still further the amount of skill that workers needed, and hence their discretion in and control over what they did. Hitherto, production generally used machinery that the operator could use to perform a variety of related tasks, which required that the operator have the necessary judgement and skill to do what was needed. At Highland Park things were different. The machines were designed to do only one job and do it very efficiently, so that the operators needed little skill and judgement. Max Wollering was one of the people at Ford involved in the design and use of these machines, and he said that, with them, "he could make a farmboy turn out work as good as that of a first-class mechanic" (Hounshell 1984: 221).

The Highland Park plant, and modern manufacturing more generally, continued a process that began when putting out started to displace cottage industry. That process marked the gradual separation of the conception of production from its execution. The household weaver producing a piece of cloth to be sold at a nearby cloth market figured out what sort of cloth he wanted to produce, which was the conception of production, and also wove it, which was the execution. The weaver did not have a free hand in these, for he was constrained by his skill and the skills of his family members, the sort of loom that he had, the nature of the yarn available and, of course, how much he thought he could charge for the different sorts of cloth that he could produce. Within these constraints, however, in consultation with his spinning wife and perhaps their children he decided what to produce and how to produce it. By the time of the Highland Park plant, all of these decisions were made by engineers and others in Ford management, the production line was laid out accordingly and workers simply performed the operations required of their station on the moving assembly line every time another piece of work appeared in front of them.

Relentless focus and rigid control were the strength of the Highland Park plant, but also its weakness. For one thing, it meant that workers were extremely alienated from their productive activities. In reaction, Ford workers quit in droves. After the installation of moving assembly lines in the Highland Park plant, labour turnover was so high that Ford had to hire more than 950 workers a year to achieve a net increase of 100; the other 850 refused to stay at their jobs (Hounshell 1984: 257–9). The company tried to deal with this by introducing what became famous: the $5 day – pay high enough to reduce turnover. In addition, the focus and control made it hard for Ford to keep up with changing fashions in automobiles, and the company switched to a more flexible system of production in the 1920s (Hounshell 1984: ch. 7).

This did not mean, however, that companies stopped trying to control workers closely to make sure that they executed faithfully the production that the firm had conceived. Rather, the controlling mechanisms became rules and procedures and systems of pay incentive, which may have given individual workers more control over their work but further weakened the bonds between them by putting them into competition with each other (e.g. Burawoy 1982).

The purpose of production

I have sketched historical changes in production, but have not focused on technological innovation and the efficiencies that it brought. Rather, I have been concerned with things that interest economic anthropologists, such as social relations among producers, control over production and relationships between producers and product. I now consider those changes in terms of another topic that interests economic anthropologists: changes in the control of the manufacturing firm itself. As I shall show, this in turn helped change the ways that some people viewed the firm and its production and the ways that they acted toward it – changes that are part of what is called financialization. Doing so means shifting the focus to those who owned the workshops, and then the factories, where production took place.

Before the Industrial Revolution, production in England that did not occur in households took place in workshops and was carried out by skilled workers, overwhelmingly men. Commonly they were members of one or another guild, which represented those who worked at the craft associated with that guild and governed how they worked and were organized.

Guild rules defined three different levels of competence: apprentice, journeyman and master. Someone who wanted to become a printer, for example, would first serve as an apprentice under a master printer, commonly for seven years. Those who completed their apprenticeship successfully would become journeymen. They were competent to pursue their craft but they were restricted in what they could do and could not take on apprentices of their own. These journeymen mostly worked in shops run by masters, and a journeyman could become a master by learning additional skills and practices, including commercial practices such as dealing with customers and suppliers. That learning was assessed when the journeyman produced a special piece of work to demonstrate his competence, called a masterpiece. Once he became a master he was entitled to set up his own workshop to exercise his craft skills, engage journeymen and take on apprentices.

In this system, those who ran businesses had risen through the ranks by mastering more and more of the technical and commercial skills associated with their craft, and their mastery justified the authority that they exercised over the journeymen and apprentices whose work they directed. This rising through the ranks was not restricted to work governed by guilds. Rather, it was common in England, as well as in the United States, as people were expected to be brought up in a trade, even if that meant only working for and learning from an uncle who was a cobbler rather than serving a formal apprenticeship.

With the increasing separation of the conception and execution of production that I described, rising through the ranks and the authority that it bestowed were less and less important. In other words, the people who produced automobiles were not the ones who designed the Highland Park plant and its machinery. That was done by people whom we would call managers, and it is pertinent that the idea that management is a distinct activity emerged around the time when the Highland Park plant was being designed. The most important early work on management, Frederick Winslow Taylor's *The Principles of Scientific Management*, appeared in 1911 (Taylor 1919 [1911]).

These new managers differed from the old guild masters, who had spent their working lives learning how to produce a particular sort of thing and practising that production and its organization. Rather, the emerging managers were not concerned with production of any particular sort, or even with organizations of any particular sort. Taylor (1919 [1911]: 8) asserted this when he said that his principles applied to "all social activities: to the management of our homes; the management of our farms; the management of the business of our tradesmen, large and small; of our churches, our philanthropic institutions, our universities, and our governmental departments". And the message about the importance of management itself, in the abstract, seems to have sunk in. A man who graduated from Harvard Business School in 1949 said:

> When most of us went to the Business School, we had no idea *what* we wanted to manage, all we knew was *that* we wanted to manage. And that seemed fine, because the way it was presented to us was that managing was a skill unto itself. [...] That was the premise that we started with, and we worked from it diligently and in some cases brilliantly. (quoted in Shames 1986: 103)

Beginning in the second half of the nineteenth century another change took place in manufacturing firms. Hitherto commonly they had been owned by an individual or a small group, in the way that guild masters owned workshops. Increasingly, however, firms became joint-stock companies, separate legal entities that sold shares to investors who collectively were seen to own the company, which was controlled by managers employed for the purpose. So, the separation of conception from execution and of management from production was joined by the separation of ownership from control (Berle & Means 1932).

Together, these changes meant that those owning and running manufacturing firms were decreasingly likely to see those firms primarily in terms of production, which was alien to managers and owners in a way that it had not been to guild masters, or even those who owned early factories. Instead, they were increasingly likely to see the firm primarily as an independent commercial entity to which they were linked in some way and that happened to produce something, and the owners were concerned that it do so at a profit.

One manifestation of this changing view in the last quarter of the twentieth century was the growing tendency to value a firm in financial terms, specifically in terms of what is called its market capitalization or market value. In this view, a firm is worth the number of its shares outstanding multiplied by the price per share, so that a firm with a million shares outstanding that trade at, say, $15 is worth $15 million. Firm management was assessed accordingly. It was deemed good if the company's market capitalization went up and was deemed bad if it went down. With this, what the firm actually produces sinks even further into the background, overshadowed by its market value and whatever would help increase it.

This change in view was hardly universal. There were firms in which workers and managers focused on their products, were proud of them and sought to make them better. There were investors, called value investors, who assessed firms and their management in terms of what the company made, how well it did so, how much it sold and how it was likely to perform in the future. Equally, however, there was growing pressure to see the firm in the financial way that I have described. This pressure was manifest in a variety of ways, usually involving a set of people, who could include senior managers, taking over the firm or threatening to do so in order to increase its market value (a fairly early instance of this is described in Burrough & Helyar 1990).

The novel way in which these people viewed firms echoed a broader cultural change in the way that at least some people viewed things in their world. I witnessed this when I was living in the United States around 1990. There was a boom in house prices in the city where I lived. People regularly told stories about how much more their house was worth than it had cost when they bought it and regularly said that they felt so much richer. In money terms they were richer, if the house that they had bought for $50,000 would now fetch $100,000. But if they viewed that house in terms of use value, as housing, a place to live of a certain size and in a certain area, then they were no better off, because it was the same as it had been when they bought it. And if they sold it during the boom they would still need a place to live, and so would have to buy another house at boom prices.

From this financial perspective, the house is little more than a crystallization of money seen as capital, by which I mean money seen as a resource that could be used to buy something that will produce yet more money, whether that is a textile factory, a second house or a work of art. Further, the factory, house or work of art is seen as a temporary crystallization, one that can be dissolved back into capital by selling it, as many people did in the United States and elsewhere in the housing bubbles that preceded the economic crisis that began in 2008.

What I have said of the changing ways that people appeared to think about housing applies as well to the ways that many speculative investors appeared to think about production. It was reduced to the exchange value of the firm doing the producing, which became a temporary crystallization of capital. In its productive operation, the firm yields a particular return on that capital. If splitting it up and selling off the bits and investing the proceeds elsewhere would produce a higher return for the owner, then it would be silly to let it continue its productive operations.

Equally, making the firm as efficient as possible in its use of resources would produce a higher return, so it would be silly to continue the older, less efficient practices. If changing the use of electricity would allow the firm to get the same things done at less cost, then the change makes sense. The same applies to the use of labour, which ceases to be the people who make things and become just another cost of production. This can, of course, have unfortunate consequences for the people who do the work, taking such forms as zero-hour contracts, subcontracting work, reductions of pay and benefits and job security, and attacks on unions. As one former employee of the Chinese firm Huawei, who got into a dispute with the company, put it, "Once a company becomes a cold, dehumanized grinding machine, what's the point for it to exist?" (quoted in Yuan 2019)

Conversely, for many economists this view of the firm is virtuous, for it is part of the rational allocation of capital in an economy, using it to produce the greatest return. That is supposed to make us all better off.

Many see financialization as a unique change that is an affliction of the modern age, or perhaps as a stage in economic evolution. Illustrating the work of economic anthropologists who are interested in larger systems, Jonathan Friedman objects to this view (e.g. 2002a, 2002b, 2013). He argues that financialization is not unique to our age but has occurred previously, and that it can have effects that are much broader than we might think.

Friedman builds on the work of Giovanni Arrighi (esp. 1994), and is concerned with the economic activities of countries and regions. To a degree his argument applies as well to specific industries in smaller places, which is an easier way to present it, and I shall do so here. Friedman says that financialization is cyclical, and occurs when capital invested in productive activities in a particular place ends up yielding a return that is less than investors will accept. To a degree, that lower return is caused by the economic success of those activities. The wealth that they produce leads to rising expectations about living standards and hence income, which increases the cost of labour and hence of production. In effect, a profitable productive activity in a given area, such as making steel in Sheffield or Pittsburgh, ends up pricing itself out of the market.

When this happens, those with capital reduce their new investment in the activity and even begin to withdraw the money that had been crystallized in the area's factories, mills and the rest. A contemporary example of this is the consequences of the reduction in US government tax on corporations in 2018, touted as a way to release money for new corporate investment. Generally the companies did not invest their additional money in any productive way, much less in things that would create jobs. They bought back their own shares, which had the effect of raising the share price and so increasing the firm's market value, and they paid higher dividends, which had the effect of returning money to investors (Krugman 2019; Tankersley *et al.* 2019). Flush with money, some individual investors spent it on opulent consumption. Others looked for new ways to invest it, including speculation in things such as art, buildings, stocks and novel financial instruments, producing asset inflation, marked by, for example, sharp increases in the price of houses, paintings by famous artists and antique cars.

Eventually, however, a new economic centre emerges, and the cycle begins again. In geographic terms, capital that was crystallized and localized because it was invested in production in a particular area ends up being dissolved and delocalized until a new area becomes a centre of productive investment, where capital again becomes crystallized and localized.

Historical evidence supports Friedman's argument that this sequence is cyclical. He shows that the textile mills in Lancashire, in England, built in the eighteenth century were financed in large part by money coming from the Middle East. The great expansion of the American railroads in the second half of the nineteenth century was paid for with substantial money from the City of London. More recently, after the First World War the textile industry in New England upped sticks and moved to the American South, where non-union workers cost much less, and textile cities such as Lowell and Fall River, Massachusetts, and Manchester, New Hampshire, lost their industrial base. In turn, in the second half of the twentieth century textile manufacturing began to move again, initially to assembly and finishing plants in the Caribbean.

Viewed as macroeconomic cycles, what Friedman describes is of no particular interest to economic anthropologists. The corollaries of those cycles are, however. For instance, the speculative boom and ostentatious consumption of the 1980s and 1990s do interest anthropologists, and Friedman's model helps account for them. He also sees broader corollaries.

Friedman argues that, when capital is crystallized and localized, the political and social influence of that capital tends to support the state, which is encouraged to protect and support the productive activities in which the capital is crystallized. This can be done by subsidies for exports, tariffs and quotas on imports, direct and indirect support for research and investment, the development of productive infrastructure, and so on. Capital's support of the state, Friedman argues, encourages a positive national identity among the citizenry, which among other things encourages a sense of commonality. Commonality is not complete, however. There is tension between capital and labour, so that political debate tends to revolve around a more labour-oriented left and a more capital-oriented right.

Things change when localized capital begins to dissolve and look for a new home. Those allied with the dissolving capital are looking for new places to invest and begin to regard the state as a hindrance. The regulation of trade that benefited capital when times were good, for instance, begins to look like a restriction of the ability of resettled manufacturing to sell its products in the country that it had abandoned. Free trade, the free movement of commodities and capital, finds increasing support and encourages globalization, at least until a new powerful centre emerges that is able to regulate trade to its advantage.

Friedman argues that this has cultural and political consequences. As the country increasingly loses the support of those who own and control capital, being cosmopolitan, not being rooted in a place, becomes more valued and the national identity that had been valued begins to be denigrated as parochial. This can affect the working class in particular ways. Members of that class generally do not benefit from the movement of capital and are attracted to the state because of the welfare and services that it provides. So, they have little reason to embrace the criticism of the country and the state that is associated with globalization and cosmopolitanism. Conversely, in the eyes of those who adhere to the values associated with capital, the working-class dislike of cosmopolitanism tends to become working-class nationalism and xenophobia, and is criticized as such. Tension between capital and labour remains, but tends to take on a different form, no longer right versus left but cosmopolitan versus local.

Thus, in her campaign for the presidency in 2016, Hillary Clinton said that "half" of Donald Trump's supporters could "be put in a basket of deplorables", those she described as "racist, sexist, homophobic, xenophobic, Islamaphobic – you name it" (Reilly 2016). It should be no surprise that "Proud to be deplorable" bumper stickers and T-shirts appeared shortly afterwards. Clinton had already appeared to ally herself with cosmopolitan capital, having taken a bit under $700,000 for three presentations to Goldman Sachs, a firm at the heart of Wall Street. The result is that many who had voted for Barack Obama previously switched to Trump, with his rhetoric that attacked people such as Clinton and that supported ordinary people dispossessed by globalization. Of those who voted for Clinton, many, like me, held their nose when they did so.

Friedman's macroeconomic cycles are a long way from Ponams, Colombian peasants and men on the Negril fishing beach. Nonetheless, they all illustrate how economic anthropologists are concerned with the different ways that people's social relations and views of the world around them shape and are shaped by productive activities. Once things are produced they circulate between people in different ways. I turn to that next.

3

Circulation, identity, relationship and order

The circulation of things from person to person is not simply a utilitarian shifting of objects from those who make them to those who want to consume them. Indeed, a lot of circulation does not even serve that utilitarian purpose. In *The Hobbit*, J. R. R. Tolkien mentions *mathom*, the hobbit name for objects of no use that people give as gifts (Tolkien 1937). These resemble the *kula* valuables that Malinowski described, things with no apparent practical purpose that circulate, seemingly endlessly, from person to person and from island to island.

Even the circulation that does not serve that useful purpose, however, is important in many areas of social life. Economic anthropologists know this, and in this chapter I describe some of the ways that it is important.

Identity and relationship

One area involves social identities and relationships. Who are we? How are we related to each other, and so how should we deal with each other? Whether they know it or not, everyone who has decided who ought to get a birthday present and what to get them or who to invite for a meal and what to serve has had to answer these questions.

On Ponam, a lot circulated in the giving and getting of daily life. It circulated in more ceremonious form in "prestations", the term for formal presentations of gifts. Bigger or smaller, there were prestations at weddings and funerals, when first fruits were gathered from an important tree, when a men's house was built or refurbished, when a woman gave birth, when a new canoe was finished and ready for launching, and on and on. Achsah Carrier and I figured that during the 13 months of our continuous fieldwork the average islander spent the equivalent of one full day out of every four or five on some prestation or other. What islanders gave and got varied little: bags of rice and sugar, bundles of dried sago flour, bags of wheat flour, tins of fish, dishes of cooked rice or sago, perhaps small amounts of cash. More important occasions, especially brideprice payments, would include special items such as carved wooden beds and belts of shell money.

At their centre, almost all the prestations had pretty much the same form. The islander making the prestation would place the items to be given on the ground, announce the reason for the gift and tell the recipient that it was now his or hers. The recipient would thank the giver and take the gift away. In a minor prestation this could take ten minutes; in a more important one it could take several hours.

If the occasion were minor and the gift small, givers would provide the gift themselves. Routinely, however, the giver would receive contributions to the gift from kin, and frequently those kin would get contributions from their kin in turn, who were likely to get contributions from yet other kin. The contributions, then, would create a web that extended out through five or six steps from the person making the prestation. This web, then, was organized differently from what I have described of the right to participate in a *lawin* expedition. There, the web was defined by descent from the ancestor whose name the right bore. This is different from the web radiating outward from the person making the prestation.

The accumulation and giving of the gift answered those questions about social identity and relationship in a number of ways. To ignorant outsiders such as Achsah Carrier and me when we started fieldwork, those answers were invisible. After a few months of watching prestations and wondering what was going on, and why so many people were paying such close attention, we came to see that the answers were blindingly obvious, even though we were never good enough to master the finer points (see Carrier & Carrier 1990).

The simplest way to explain things is with what islanders called *sahai*. That was a distribution that normally consisted of dishes of cooked food, and it always went to *kamal*, agnatic groups that owned real property, land and perhaps sea. People had *sahai* on two sorts of occasions. One was those in which *kamal* were especially important, such as the refurbishment of a *kamal* men's house. The other was when they wanted to give to islanders generally, and, since every Ponam was a member of one or another *kamal*, in a *sahai* everyone ended up with a share.

In a *sahai* the sets of dishes of cooked food were laid out in two lines. A speaker would walk down one line, point to each of the sets in turn and announce which *kamal* it was for, and then do the same with the other line. Although it took a while to figure it out, the two lines were a map of Ponam *kamal*, and the *sahai* was an answer to the question of who islanders were.

The map could have been straightforward, because *kamal* men's houses were arrayed in two rough lines, one on the northern half of the island and one on the southern. The sets of dishes could have been laid out in the order in which one would encounter them if one walked from one end of the village to the other. Such an arrangement would have been dull, however. What made the displays interesting was that they reflected people's assessments of what really were Ponam *kamal* and where they really were located – assessments that are social rather than geographical and that were answers to the question of how people were related to each other.

Although each men's house could be located on a map, it was not clear that all were in their proper places. For example, one *kamal* had been founded at a site on the northern half of the island, but a few generations ago a combination of pressure on village land and disagreements among kin led *kamal* members to move their men's house to a piece of land in the southern half that some of their relatives allowed them to use. This geographic inconsistency did not bother people, however, who routinely put the dishes for this *kamal* in the line for the northern half at the spot where the men's house had been previously.

Before colonization late in the nineteenth century a different *kamal* had existed well to the east of where the village was located when we were there. Because of pre-colonial warfare, that part of the island was abandoned and this *kamal* built its men's house in the village. The leader of the *kamal* wanted to return it to its ancestral location, and by the time of fieldwork had persuaded his *kamal*-mates to build their men's house there, even though they did not want to live in the bush away from the village. The leader had a job in Port Moresby, the country's capital, and was on Ponam only when he returned for his Christmas leave. In *sahai* that took place when he was on the island his *kamal*'s share was placed at the easterly end of the northern line, reflecting where the men's house was and where he wanted it to be. To the amusement of islanders, when he was away the share was nestled in among the shares of other northern *kamal*, where his *kamal*-mates wanted to be.

There were cases in which the *kamal*'s place in *sahai* was less amusing and more contentious. Two *kamal* were in an uncertain relationship. One asserted that past generosity made it the dominant member of the pair; members of the other rejected this. Those who set out the dishes in *sahai* had to decide whether they would side with the *kamal* that claimed dominance or reject the claim. Those who rejected it placed the sets of dishes for the two *kamal* according to their physical locations on the island, which were separated by other *kamal*. Those who accepted the claim placed the two sets next to each other. So, those who laid out *sahai* were stating how different sets of people were related to each other and hence how they ought to deal with each other.

Sahai also required organizers to decide which sets of people were a *kamal* and which were not. A *kamal* was supposed to be the agnatic descendants of the founder, but there was one *kamal* that had no surviving men. Its last member was an old widow, who, in accordance with Ponam rules, had taken on her husband's *kamal* membership when she married, and she looked after *kamal* property. She had no sons. Her daughters, all married and so members of other *kamal*, helped her. Another *kamal* included the agnatic descendants of a man who had been taken in and looked after during the same warfare that had led the *kamal* mentioned earlier to abandon its original site and move to the village. Those taken in and looked after in that way were treated as *kamal* members but were subordinate to those who took them in. That set of descendants chafed at their subordinate status, sought their independence as a separate *kamal* and had a building that they said was their men's house.

Those setting out *sahai* had to decide. Would they be the first to leave out the *kamal* with no surviving men? Would they be the first to include that set of men asserting their independence? *Kamal* membership is important for answering the question of who Ponams are, and there was agreement about what made a *kamal*. It was in the giving and getting of *sahai*, however, that islanders had to decide the borderline cases and declare which people really were a *kamal* and which were not.

What islanders did was not unique to them or to subsistence societies such as theirs. In their giving, people in the United States and the United Kingdom also identify who they are, how they are related to each other and how they ought to deal with each other. And, as with Ponams, this is visible in ceremonious giving: Christmas, of course, but also occasions such as birthdays, graduations, weddings, the birth of children, retirement and funerals. I look at some aspects of this.

A few years ago my elder son took up with a lady friend, and, although I knew of her existence, I had not met her. I am not good at picking presents for my children, and, since my son lived in the same city as me, for his birthday I would give him a meal out with me and my wife at a restaurant of his choice. The question was what to do about the lady friend. Did she get invited too? To do so is to treat her developing relationship with my son as also a relationship with his parents – in effect, to begin to treat her as one of the family, with all that this implies. The same problem appeared at Christmas. Does she get nothing? Does she get a standard gift, such as a box of chocolates? Does she get something personal, an idea that my son comes up with when I ask him what she would like? Like a *sahai* on Ponam, the ceremonious giving to my son and his lady friend helps answer the question of how we are related and how we ought to deal with each other.

The second aspect of ceremonious giving is more complicated, and it concerns what to give. In the United States and the United Kingdom people generally hold that a proper gift to a person in a personal relationship should be personal and thoughtful, rather than being hurriedly pulled off the shop shelf at the last minute or something that your secretary selected on your behalf. In the 1840s Ralph Waldo Emerson (1983 [1844]: 95–6) stressed the need for personality in an uncompromising way in what he said of gifts of "compliment and love":

> The only gift is a portion of thyself. Thou must bleed for me. Therefore the poet brings his poem; the shepherd, his lamb; the farmer, corn; the miner, a gem; the sailor, coral and shells; the painter, his picture; the girl, a handkerchief of her own sewing. This is right and pleasing, for it restores societies in so far to its primary basis, when a man's biography is conveyed in a gift.

In those countries people also commonly think that money is about as impersonal as a thing can be, and so unsuited for giving in a personal relationship. Appropriately, a gift of money is rare among parents and children, and when it does occur normally it is from parents to their children. Further, often the gift is treated as not really money, for it is expected that it will be memorialized in objects. That is, it is seen as a contribution to a substantial purchase, such as household furnishings. Money is common, however, in gifts given at Christmas to those related to the giver in impersonal, even somewhat commercial, ways. People who live in apartment houses will give money to staff. When I first moved to the United Kingdom, years ago, I learned to give money at Christmas to those who collected the rubbish and delivered the mail.

The third aspect of ceremonious giving is a concern with equivalence, the equality of the value of what people give each other. In his study of Middletown, Theodore Caplow (1984) found that there was little or no concern for equivalence within the immediate family, between the couple and between them and their children. Things were different, however, with gifts to and from collaterals and their spouses, which means siblings, sibling's spouses and children, parents' siblings. He found that people were clearly concerned that gifts to and from these people should be roughly equal. For those more distant yet, concern for equivalence disappears. We do not expect that the gift given at office parties, much less to those who deliver the mail, will produce an equivalent return.

In this, Middletown resembles what Marshall Sahlins (1974) says of reciprocity in societies of the Western Pacific. There are three sorts. One is generalized, dominant in one's immediate group, with little or no concern that the giving and getting are equal. The second is balanced, dominant at the edges of the group, with a concern for equivalence. The third is negative, dominant in dealings with strangers, with a concern to get as much as one can, perhaps through sharp practice and even theft.

It appears, then, that the circulation of things on birthdays, graduation and the like is not simply the movement of objects of more or less exchange and use value. Of course those objects have those values, and we could calculate the giving on those occasions in economistic terms. If we ignored the value but kept the economic focus on individuals and their desires, we might think that the gifts are just expressions of the giver's thought about the recipient, and in spite of all the evidence we do tell ourselves that it is the thought that counts. If we broaden our interest to include the social side of things, however, we can see that they are not simply expressions but in fact are communications that involve the giver and the recipient, and hence the relationship between them.

To some degree, that is what is called a gift relationship – long a topic of interest to economic anthropologists. The classic consideration is by Marcel Mauss (1990 [1925]). He said that a person in such a relationship is obliged to give a gift in the appropriate circumstances (such as graduation or a birthday), to receive such a gift and to reciprocate at the appropriate time. For Mauss, then, the gift is not a free and spontaneous expression of sentiment. Rather, it is an obligation, and failure to meet it without a very good reason brings criticism, even anger. Mauss presented this obligation in terms of what had been described for the Maori, of New Zealand. For them, he said, the gift contained a spirit, *hau*, which would harm those who denied the obligation to reciprocate.

Malinowski described how such relationships can develop in his work on the *kula*. *Kula* transactions are between partners from different places, who give each other valuables as part of their gift relationship. That relationship begins when a *kula* trader decides that he wants to have another trader become a partner. He then engages in what looks a lot like courtship. That is, he gives the hoped-for partner a series of initiatory gifts called *vaga*. They are freely given, in the sense that they reflect no existing obligation but only the trader's desire. If the *vaga* gifts produce the desired result, the recipient will in time present the giver with a *kula* valuable – the beginning of their partnership: their gift relationship.

Much has been written trying to explain why this sort of initiatory giving so often leads to a gift relationship. The conclusion seems to be something along the lines of "I don't know. It just does." Or, as Sahlins (1974: 186) puts it: "If friends make gifts, gifts make friends."

Ponam prestations show how circulation can produce and reproduce social identities and relationships. Like prestations in the United States and the United Kingdom, they did so in stable surroundings. Although I mentioned raiding on the island, there was no fighting in the area after around 1920.

Moka, peace and order

Things were different in the New Guinea Highlands. The area had a long history of warfare among autonomous groups and villages, and what was called "tribal fighting" continued through the 1980s. There was no state or other overarching institution that enforced peace and good order, but there were social practices that moderated a Hobbesian war of all against all, and the circulation of objects was important among them.

Economic anthropologists have described two, linked ways that it did so. One is competitive systems of exchange, such as what the Highland group the Melpa called *moka*, described by Andrew Strathern (1971). The other is the ways that people accumulated and used items for those exchanges – part of what is called the "big man" system, analysed by Marshall Sahlins (1963, 1974). In both of these, circulation was important for creating relationships that produced a degree of social and political peace, however fragile, in a region where those were scarce.

Stripped of its ceremony, subtleties and tactics, *moka* is straightforward. At least, it is so for those familiar with exchange systems in the Western Pacific, which is likely to leave out most of those who are reading this. I have tried to accommodate those readers by presenting only the basic logic of the system and avoiding Melpa terms other than *moka* itself. Even with that, however, what follows will strike some as technical and dense. It will, however, give some sense of the complexity of what economic anthropologists often confront.

Commonly, *moka* began with what is called marriage exchange, which has two parts. The first was a prestation, with its associated speeches and festivities, made by the groom's side to the bride's around the time of marriage. The second, at some later date, was a return prestation from the bride's side to the groom's, and it was proportional to the initial prestation. These prestations were not ad hoc affairs but involved substantial communication and coordination between the leaders of the two sides to ensure that the event went off smoothly. In any event, formally that second prestation ended the marriage exchange. The man leading the bride's side could, however, make a return prestation that was in excess of what was expected. In that case, the man who received the return prestation (and those who made *moka* were men) became indebted to the giver.

At this point, three things were possible. First, if the recipient did not repay the excess he would remain in debt to the giver and so be inferior to him, without prestige or repute in a society in which these were important. Second, he could make a return payment equal to the amount of the excess. In that case, neither party would be in debt to the other, their status would not change and their transactions would be complete. Third, the recipient, the leader of the groom's side in the original marriage prestation, could make a return prestation that was larger than the excess, and his repute would rise.

In that case, the leader of the bride's side would have the same choices that I have just described: he could make no return, he could make a return equal to the excess, he could make a return larger than the excess. If he did the last, the cycle would continue for another turn.

The system, then, was one of alternating disequilibrium. First one *moka* player and then the other gained ascendancy by giving a return gift larger than needed to reciprocate what he had received, thereby putting his *moka* partner in his debt. Systems such as *moka* are interesting in themselves. Here, however, what is important is what goes on around the prestations that the two men made to each other, for it is there that some degree of political and social peace was created.

Those who were serious players were involved in a number of *moka* relationships, and these often formed a chain or, as in the title of Strathern's book, a rope. Consider the leader of the groom's side, whom I call B. He was the one who received that return prestation from the leader of the bride's side, whom I call A, that contained the original excess. When he received it, he found himself possessed of a mass of valuables. If he was able and fortunate, he could arrange things so that he passed these on in due course to person C as part of a *moka* payment to him. If C also was able and fortunate, he could pass them on to D, and so on. And, when D eventually made a return prestation to C, C would be able to do the same to B, who could use the valuables to make a return prestation to A, who had started all this off.

It is chains or ropes such as this that helped bring about social peace in the Highlands. The *moka* players A and C may have lived a fair distance from each other, and, before the imposition of colonial control, travel to places where you were a stranger was dangerous – as it remained in parts of the Highlands into the 1970s and beyond. Our A, on the other hand, was known to B, who could vouch for him to C, and so on down the chain. The circulation that is *moka* did not make the Highlands peaceful and orderly. For those so inclined, however, it was the basis for a degree of security, enough for at least some people to travel well beyond nearby villages in relative safety.

Another aspect of that circulation did the same, only this time in the more limited area defined by those who supported a *moka* player.

Highland societies generally were organized by kinship, with patrilineal descent groups of varying sizes. The basic ones were fairly small and local, perhaps no more than a handful of people in a single village. These would be subordinate parts of larger descent groups, but the larger the groups the less likely they were to be coherent and able to act as a unit. Indeed, smaller groups within the same larger unit could be enemies, occasionally to the point of armed conflict. So, the absence of social order that existed at the regional level existed at a fairly local level as well.

The hypothetical *moka* that I described above began with marriage prestations between the side of the groom and that of the bride. Such prestations were not very large, and potential *moka* players drew on their near kin for contributions to their prestations, as was the case with prestations on Ponam. For energetic and successful players, however, the brideprice prestation was only the beginning.

Such players sought to become what are called "big men", seeking the renown that came from being successful. Seeking success meant hard work, which only increased with achievement. An aspiring big man sought to establish *moka* relationships with a number of other players; the more renown, the better. This required skill at, and attention to, negotiations with those players about the timing of prestation, what would be given, who would be asked to attend, and so on.

It also required accumulating the valuables to be given, a process that enhanced social cohesion. Valuables included durable items such as decorated shells and ceremonial axes. The more important thing that they included was not so durable: pigs. In a prestation of any consequence, a substantial number of live pigs were part of the prestation, and a smaller number were cooked and eaten as part of the festivities associated with it. In the subsistence societies of the Highlands, there were only two legitimate ways to get pigs. One could be given them or rear them. However one acquired them, they required land on which to graze and to grow food for them, normally yams, and the labour to tend them and their food crops. *Moka* players worked hard at recruiting others to do some of the work involved.

Initially they were likely to be his wife or wives and his sisters, all of whom had other demands on their time. For a prestation of any size he had to look further afield, usually still among kin: his sisters' husbands, but also those more distantly related. With their support, he might have been able to mount a successful minor *moka* prestation and begin to be noticed more widely. His success gratified those who assisted him and made it easier for him to establish other *moka* relationships and attract further supporters. If, some time later, he mounted a larger prestation to a more prominent big man he was on his way to becoming a prominent big man himself, with the renown and influence that came with it.

This meant that he had more demands made on him and needed more supporters. He could not secure them by invoking kinship obligations, for the pool of potential supporters was likely to include only non-kin or those very distantly related to him. Instead, he had to induce them to help. One way to do this was to give a few piglets to a potential supporter, who took on the work of rearing them and was expected to surrender the grown pigs to the player when he needed them. This meant that our player needed a supply of piglets and, in due course, would need something to reward the people who reared them.

Demands became more insistent when our player received a *moka* prestation from someone else in return for one that he had made. That meant that he had valuables, but also many uses for them. Some went as reward to those who supported his earlier prestation, for which he had received this return; some went as inducements to those who he hoped to recruit as supporters for a future prestation. Some might go as partial return to those to whom he had an outstanding *moka* debt and some might go as an initial part of a prestation that he wanted to make to another player in the future.

In this circulation to past and future supporters and *moka* players, the aspiring big man created a set of obligations and relationships. These were unlike what occurred in Ponam prestations, which rested on a set of existing kin relationships. Rather, they cut across kinship lines, and the more successful the big man, the more they did so. The successful big man, then, was the focus of a social network of reciprocal obligation based on past and future *moka* prestations, a network in which his supporters could enjoy the fellowship of their support for him and share his renown, and one that was a sphere of sociality and relative harmony that was larger than those small, local patrilines.

This harmony was unstable, however. A big man held no office, and so had no established authority. He could only persuade people to support him. In addition, the *moka* system was competitive, with no defined goal or end point. Each player tried to give ever larger gifts to an ever greater number of partners of ever more prestige and so gain ever more renown. Consequently, big men were under recurring pressure to use what they received in prestations to attract new supporters and make *moka* with new partners, and so give their existing supporters less than what they thought was their due. If that happened, the big man's supporters would abandon him and he would fail – no longer a big man but a rubbish man.

Moreover, there was no obvious way out. A big man who wanted to retire from the game with his reputation intact would need to repay all his *moka* debts to existing partners, and those repayments would not be reciprocated. With no promise of future reward, supporters would be unhappy, and less likely to take the piglets and rear them and to do all the other work that was needed. Big men, then, did not retire. Instead, they were defeated. They lost renown, and the network of order that centred on them disappeared.

Thus it is, then, that *moka* and its big men generated a degree of cohesion and security in a fairly anarchic and even violent part of the world. As stated above, however, big men and their networks and relationships were unstable. This is because big men were only as good as their last performance, a function of their skill, luck and energy. In different circumstances a leader's position and the associated cohesion could rest on a more solid footing and a different form of circulation.

Controlling circulation

One set of those circumstances is associated with one of the three main forms of circulation that Polanyi described: redistribution. I present this more briefly than *moka* because its elements are likely to seem more familiar to readers. In it, a leader collected contributions from people, pooled them and distributed them back to those people. This implies that leaders have a degree of authority, which justifies their requesting or even demanding such contributions and deciding how to distribute them. That authority is an important difference between such systems and things such as *moka*. A *moka* player, as I have said, could only induce support, not command it, and his discretion in how he distributed valuables was severely constrained by the expectation of his supporters and *moka* partners.

This discretion in redistribution systems meant that what people received from the leader was not their right, either the social right of contributors to a *moka* prestation to a share of the return or the right by law of a citizen to distributions from government. In the United States, after all, social security payments are defined by a set of rules laid down in and justified by various acts of Congress, just as in the United Kingdom the existence and nature of access to the National Health Service is a matter of law. Neither one's monthly social security cheque nor one's ability to visit one's GP is seen to depend on the whim or favour of an official.

Because of this discretion, what people get in a system of redistribution is to some degree a gift of the leader, which ties the recipients to the leader and solidifies his or her authority. Sahlins (1974: 133) reports that there is an Eskimo saying about the relationship between these distributions and authority: "Gifts make slaves as whips make dogs".

The authority that leaders in redistribution systems have, and that *moka* players lack, can rest on a variety of things, but often they involve descent in some way. The authority can come from the leader having a special spiritual power or grace, itself arising from being the child of a previous leader. Equally, it can rest on descent pure and simple, as in hereditary monarchy. In such cases, the relationship between leader and followers may also be presented in terms of kinship, though often of a fictitious or symbolic sort – the way that George Washington is the "father" of his country. This is not the affectionate kinship that people celebrate in the United Kingdom and the United States, for the relationships involved are clearly unequal. They are that of the paterfamilias and the subordinate members of his household.

I have said that leaders in systems of redistribution have authority that is likely to rest on cultural understandings – things such as descent and what passes from parents to children. Some argue, however, that it may be wrong to see cultural factors as justifying the authority that leaders have, authority that allows them to shape the flow of wealth. Those people argue that we may have things backward: it is not the authority that underlies the leader's control of circulation, but it is the control of circulation that underlies the leader's authority.

This argument raises a question, however. Beliefs about authority, whether of the beneficent slave owner, of the monarch, of the sacred leader or even of the rightful owner, take time to become established. If this authority becomes accepted because of the leader's control of the flow of wealth, how is it that a person or group has control over that flow that is sufficiently secure and long-lasting that cultural beliefs bestowing authority can become established?

What I have said of *moka* and big men illustrates the question. A successful big man might well be the point of intersection of different *moka* chains, and it is conceivable that he could try to manipulate the flow of wealth passing along those chains in order to secure his ascendancy over others and, perhaps, make himself a point of redistribution. Big men were dependent on the efforts of their supporters, however, whom they had to induce. Their attempts to manipulate the flow of wealth in such a way likely would lead to disaffection among supporters and a future as a rubbish man.

Writing about a different area in New Guinea, Ron Brunton (1975) suggests an answer. That area is the Trobriand Islands, where Malinowski did his fieldwork. Unlike the Highlands – or, for that matter, most of the region – societies in the Trobriands have chiefs. Also unlike the Highlands and most of the region, the Trobriands are small islands fairly distant from each other. This means that there was substantial sea-going trade, like the *kula* voyages that Malinowski described. This trade was not easy, but required substantial resources, coordination among people and links with traders on other islands. Brunton argues that those who were successful in this trade formed an elite, who passed their seafaring knowledge and skills, and their links with traders on other islands, down to their children. Over the course of time these elites became chiefly clans that claimed to possess, and were seen to possess, special chiefly substance that set them off from ordinary people.

Brunton's argument, then, is that accidents of geography can produce a situation in which some members of a society have a degree of control over circulation. If they can turn that control to their advantage, they may be able to maintain it long enough for beliefs and practices to develop that turn the control into legitimate authority. After all, geography and the trade that it channels changes much more slowly than does the rise and fall of big men.

This sort of thing is not restricted to the islands to the east of New Guinea. The Rhine is fairly navigable from Switzerland to the North Sea. From the modern town of Bingen am Rhein downstream to below Koblenz, the river runs through a series of gorges, and boats were vulnerable to attack from people on the shore. Many of those on the shore were happy to threaten force unless the boat gave them money, and they were paid. The geography of this part of the Rhine did not change much over the past couple of thousand years, so those shore people had plenty of time to develop arguments and beliefs that turned their extortion into legitimate ownership of part of the river and the right to collect tolls from those who wanted to use it. The result is a set of castles overlooking the Rhine, such as Marksburg, and UNESCO designating that part of the river a World Heritage Site.

We could say that something similar occurred with changes in commercial and economic practice in the United States and the United Kingdom in the eighteenth and nineteenth centuries, although the pertinent features are political and economic rather than geographic. I described some of those changes in the preceding chapter and I describe others in a subsequent chapter. Those changes involved new sets of people coming to control important aspects of the economy: merchant and industrial capitalists, who engaged in new forms of circulation that benefited them at the expense of others. Their increasing control was facilitated by government policies, and generated significant popular resistance (for these in England, see Polanyi 1944; Thompson 1971). That control was sufficiently secure, however, that it allowed the development of a set of beliefs that justified it, and so furthered that control: part of liberal economics. The justification centred on the belief that an unfettered market and capitalists seeking the greatest profit resulted in the most efficient allocation of capital, making us all better off.

This is, then, a belief that there is a system underlying economic activity, and that a laissez-faire policy benefits that system and all who live in it. One corollary is that those who are most involved in the system are the most knowledgeable about it and are, like those Trobriand chiefs, endowed with a special something that gives them authority and justifies their actions. Thus, Lloyd Blankfein, who was the head of a key firm in the system, Goldman Sachs, could say, only somewhat ironically, that his firm was "doing God's work" (DealBook 2009). As Karen Ho (2009: chs 1, 2) describes in her study of Wall Street, those in the financial sector came to believe that they were brighter and better able than ordinary people to see how things work and thus knew when the rules should be followed and when they should not. As she summarizes this view, "Bankers are allowed to break the rules because they are superior beings" (Ho 2012: 423).

In this view, the system is sufficiently important that it justifies making sacrifices to ensure that it operates properly – sacrifices guided by the financial sector, which knows the system best. A man who worked in an investment bank expressed this nicely: "Inefficiency requires reallocation of assets. That includes people, and that can be painful, especially if you are one of the people. But society as a whole is still, without question, better off" (quoted in Ho 2012: 420).

We have moved away from redistribution, but have pursued the implications of one aspect of such systems. That is the relationship between control over circulation and authority, and especially Brunton's suggestion that authority – the use of power that is seen to be legitimate – follows from that control. In this way, sea-going Trobriand traders become chiefs, powerful people on the Rhine's shores become legitimate owners of parts of the river and, in a different way, investment bankers become the agents of God.

4

Gifts and commodities

I have described what Karl Polanyi called the formalist approach to economy, effectively neoclassical economics: a concern with people allocating their limited resources between alternative ends. Economists call those ends "preferences", take them as given and do not investigate them, or even really care about them. This is most obvious in their approach to markets. There, a mass of people with a variety of preferences and a range of resources are treated as an undifferentiated mass called something such as "market demand". All that seems to be important is the transaction of money for objects. In the preceding chapter I showed the way that something else concerns many economic anthropologists: the ways that the circulation of objects reflects and affects social identities and relationships. For Marcel Mauss, and for anthropologists generally, objects that circulate in this way are called gifts, while objects that circulate in an impersonal market are called commodities.

This anthropological use of the term "commodity" is different from the Marxian use. There, as I noted previously, what is important about a commodity is not the sort of transactions in which it circulates but, instead, that it is produced with the intention of selling it, such as the cloths described in Chapter 2 (see Carrier 2018a). Further, in the market such commodities commonly are fetishized. This means that they are presented, and seen, as bearers of use and exchange value that are stripped of the processes and relations by means of which they are produced and brought to our consideration. On a supermarket shelf the bottle of soft drink tells us that it is cool and refreshing and its price is displayed. Nothing, however, tells us about the people who thought it up and made it, the drivers who brought it to the store or the assistants who put it on the shelf.

The anthropological use of "commodity" differs as well from common use, which shares that fetishism. In that use the term refers to an object that is mass-produced and with few or no distinguishing features, such as table salt or plain white T-shirts. Firms do not want to make or sell such things, but commonly seek to distinguish their wares in some way. They try to make them singularities that, they hope, will give them an advantage in a competitive market. If they have been in business a long time, their company name or brand may be enough. They may also try to associate their wares with one or another attribute or value that does not change the material properties of the product itself but, they hope, will give it a glamour that will increase demand.

Turning a commodity into a singularity can involve associating it with a celebrity of some sort or with other social images that are thought to be attractive. Although these images may be social, they are impersonal, in the sense that they are not people with whom potential purchasers interact. The sprinter portrayed in an advertisement for a running shoe may be someone we know of, but is unlikely to be someone we know.

As with "commodity", the anthropological use of the term "gift" also departs from ordinary usage. There, a gift is something that one person gives to another consciously as a present and with some degree of ceremony – what I have been calling a prestation. The object given might be wrapped and tied with a bow, and the giver is likely to announce that it is a present, whether saying "Happy birthday" or "Here's something I got for you when I was in London". For most economic anthropologists, gifts are not defined by the ribbon, ceremony and talk but by the relationship in which they move.

If some friends go to a bar on Friday evening and one buys a round of drinks for all of them, the drinks are a gift from the person who bought them, as will be the second round of drinks that another member of the group buys. Even less ceremonious, if I cook dinner I am giving my wife the work of my cooking, just as she earlier gave me the work of her shopping when she bought what I use to prepare the meal. In the bar and the house, things given move within fairly durable social relationships, and they move in both directions, as each gives similar things to others in the relationship.

This is different from what happens when one of the friends got that round of drinks and when my wife did her shopping in the supermarket. She and the friend are likely to have no social relationship with the check-out assistant at the supermarket or the person behind the bar. For them, in addition, different things move only in one direction, and normally in return for money. The friend always gets drinks from the person behind the bar in return for money. My wife never gets money from the check-out assistant in return for groceries.

Obligation, alienation, relationship

Although Mauss produced the classic description of gifts and commodities, the most thorough modern consideration of them is by C. A. Gregory (1980, 1982). It reflects his interest in settings where colonizers bring conventional markets and transactions, and confront local people to whom they are alien. Appropriately, Gregory is concerned with gift systems and commodity systems, although he says that any given society is likely to have both, to different degrees, interacting with each other.

Commodity and gift systems are oriented differently. The former is concerned with the social reproduction of things, the latter with the social reproduction of people. The social reproduction of things means the social organization of production and circulation, such as factories and markets, with the attendant social differentiation, such as different classes, levels of consumption and the like. It also means the reproduction of the social identity of objects as commodities and the different ways that people are related to them.

The social reproduction of people includes their social organization and relationships. These can be more formal and ascriptive, such as clans and age sets, but also less so, such as clubs, local sports teams or even friends who regularly meet at the bar after work on Fridays. As these examples indicate, those organizations and relationships can be more or less durable and more or less important in people's lives. The social reproduction of people also means people's social identities, both in terms of those organizations and relationships and in terms of what it means to be a person.

People transact objects in both these systems, but do so in different ways, which can be distinguished in terms of three things: the degree to which transacting is voluntary; the nature of the link between what is transacted and those who transact it; and the way that the transactors are linked to each other. As will become clear, the distinction between gift and commodity systems is not simply analytical but resembles a cultural distinction common in the West. Gift systems are close to the way that people think that home and family, and social life more generally, ought to be, while commodity systems echo thoughts about employment and market transactions, and economic life more generally.

Obligation

People in commodity systems do not produce what they need to survive but have to get it in transactions with others. These transactions are free, however. So long as you have the money you can buy your groceries at any store you like, and you can sell your labour power to anyone who wants to employ you. Conversely, in gift systems transactions are obligatory. We need to give the appropriate things to the appropriate people on the appropriate occasions. This is not a formal obligation and we will not be arrested if we fail to meet it. Your dereliction will be noticed, however, and you will be censured if you do not have a good reason why you did not buy a round of drinks when it was your turn or did not give your daughter a present on her birthday.

Further, transactions in these two systems have different effects. In commodity systems completing the transaction dissolves the relationship between transactors. Once you pay the check-out assistant for your groceries the two of you are done with each other. Once you pay off the loan, you and the bank can walk away from each other. In gift systems, however, completing the transaction does something different, which Marshall Sahlins points to when he says that gifts make friends. When you buy the second round of drinks in the bar, you have reciprocated the drink that your friend bought you, and in doing so you have recreated your relationship, reaffirmed that you are friends who buy each other drinks. The relationship may not be as intense as that between lovers or people in the same Highlands clan segment, but it is different from the relationship between you and the check-out assistant.

As this suggests, what it means to be a person differs in the two systems. In commodity systems people are expected to be autonomous, linked only at the moment of transaction. Indeed, they are supposed to be independent of each other, for only if they are, only if they transact at arm's length, can they look after their own interests properly. The situation is reversed in gift systems. Strangers do not buy each other rounds of drinks or give each other birthday presents, which would be an intrusion in people's personal lives. Friends do, however, and so affirm that they are part of a "we" that to some degree subsumes each one's separate "I".

This shows again how an economistic view of gift transactions, with its attention to individual calculation of gains and losses, is inadequate. The gains and losses are there. When a man prepares dinner for his family, they can eat for less than they could at a restaurant. But this does not explain why he cooks the meal, why his family accepts it and how their actions affect their relationship and the ways that they deal with each other in the future.

Alienation

Mauss said that objects in gift relations are not alienated but are durably linked to the people who possess them and who transact them. Even though in common law the gift belongs solely to the recipient, the link is there. Because of this, the scarf that your mother gave you is different from an identical scarf on display in a store. She selected it for you, so that it carries her identity and relationship with you and the occasion of the giving. In this, that scarf is like the valuables given in *kula* transactions that Malinowski described. There, the necklaces and armbands have histories of those who possessed and transacted them in the past, in the same way that family heirlooms have in the tales of those who first acquired them and how they were passed down the generations.

The association of person and object means that it is not only the person who possesses the object. Additionally, the object possesses the person, for the identities and relations that it embodies help to define the possessor as one who stands in this particular relationship with these particular people and so is part of a "we". This is most obvious when things go wrong. If the scarf from my mother were the wrong colour and design, I would not want to throw it out, for rejecting the gift would mean rejecting the giver and the giving. Appropriately, advice columnists in newspapers occasionally suggest how to deal with unwanted gifts – advice that they never offer about how to deal with paperbacks bought at airport bookshops that turn out to be boring.

Objects transacted in commodity relations are different. They are bundles of use and exchange value, with perhaps an overlay of impersonal symbolism such as youth, sporting ability or even the identity of a famous person (whom, as I have said, we have never met). They are assessed accordingly. If the bottle of wine that you buy does not please you, you can pour it down the drain without a thought, which you would not do if the same bottle of wine were given you by your son.

This means that in commodity systems objects are alienated from those who transact them. Once Fred pays his money, the store where he bought his jacket has no claim on it or on the warmth that it provides. Moreover, so long as the jacket is as advertised, Fred has no claim on the store or the assistant who sold it to him. As we are warned, *caveat emptor*. Of course Fred may like the jacket and the store and decide to shop there in the future, but this is his personal choice, not a social obligation in the way that he is obliged to continue to exchange anniversary presents with his wife.

Being impersonal bundles of use and exchange value, objects in commodity system are fungible, meaning that one can be replaced by another of the same class. Newspapers, candy bars and oil are fungible. When they buy a copy of today's city edition of *The New York Times*, a Dairy Milk chocolate bar or 1,000 barrels of West Texas Intermediate crude, people do not complain that they got this copy, this bar or this thousand barrels rather than that one, for all are assumed to be the same. This is the result of mass production, whereby all the copies of the newspaper that come off the presses are the same, as it is the basis of product advertising, which touts the virtue of Dairy Milk bars as a class of thing, not this or that particular one.

I have presented the personality and impersonality of objects and transactions in stylized terms, as an all-or-none affair, but the real world is not this simple. We distinguish bread made in an industrial facility on the outskirts of town from that made in a small bakery a few blocks away from where we live, although we may not be able to taste the difference when they are toasted and buttered. Equally, we prefer to buy our jackets from assistants who are friendly and attentive rather than from those who are impersonally efficient, even if the jackets and the prices are the same. This is a sign of a point that I made earlier and will return to later: the anthropological distinction between gifts and commodities resembles the common cultural distinction between social and economic realms of life.

People appear to value things that seem social – the local loaf and the friendly assistant – even though they are not really social. One of the reasons why they are not is that they come without the recurrent interactions and obligations that are part of actual social relationships. Another reason, as Arlie Hochschild (1983) describes in her study of airline cabin crew, is that seeming social is part of some people's job. The attentive and friendly assistants are paid to be that way, and may be fired if they are not. In this way, the assistants are not only alienated from what they sell, from the customer and from the transaction. In a sense they are also alienated from themselves, for their friendly attention need be no expression of themselves. It is just a part of their jobs, donned at the start of the working day and abandoned at the end.

I said that my discussion of gift and commodity systems and relationships echoes common Western cultural understandings of the social and economic realms, and those understandings are interesting for their substance and their exaggerations. The exaggerations arise because the understandings distinguish those realms from each other and define them dialectically, each in opposition to the other. David Schneider has written a lot about these two elements of culture as they exist in the United States. He calls them "home" and "work", roughly what I have called "society" and "economy". He writes: "The family as a symbol is a pattern for how kinship relations should be conducted; the opposition between 'home' and 'work' defines these meanings quite clearly and states them in terms of the features which are distinctive to each and opposed to the other" (Schneider 1980: 45). In these two realms, people see themselves in different ways: in terms of who you are as a person and in terms of your performance of specific tasks. Talcott Parsons, perhaps the leading American sociologist of the middle of the twentieth century, contrasted the two realms when he wrote:

> Broadly speaking, there is no sector of our society where the dominant patterns stand in sharper contrast to those of the occupational world than in the family. The family is a solidary group within which status, rights, and obligations are defined primarily by membership as such and by the ascribed differentiations of age, sex, and biological relatedness. This basis of relationship and status in the group precludes more than a minor emphasis on universalistic standards of functional performance. Similarly,

the patterning of rights and obligations in the family is not restricted to the context specific to a positively defined functional role; rather, it is functionally diffuse. [...] Finally, instead of being defined in impersonal, emotionally neutral terms, the family is specifically treated as a network of emotionally charged relationships, the mutual affection of its members in our society being held to be the most important basis of their solidarity and loyalty. (Parsons 1959: 262)

Schneider makes the same point with more punch: "Home is not kept for money and, of those things related to home and family, it is said that there are some things that money can't buy! The formula in regard to work is exactly reversed at home: What is done is done for love, not for money! And it is love, of course, that money can't buy" (Schneider 1980: 46).

Given this cultural opposition, it is no surprise that people routinely tell themselves that the economic realm is what the economists say it is, full of calculating individuals who know the price of everything and the value of nothing, even though they may know that their boss is a decent person, that some of their co-workers are their friends and that the local shop they have been using for years has nice, thoughtful staff. They also tell themselves that the family, the quintessence of the social realm, is a haven in a heartless world, where relationships are close and loving, even though they may barely be on speaking terms with their adolescent daughter and see their parents only once a year, if that.

Presenting these two realms in stark, ideal-typical terms simplifies things, which is useful. It allows us to see the basic principles, logic and practices of gift and commodity, society and economy, home and work. Doing so provides a perspective that encourages us to see things around us afresh, like the attentive assistant and the local loaf. It also allows us to see how different, specific cases can lie on a continuum between these two poles.

The continuum does not exist only at the level of us and those local shops. It exists as well among large firms. Ronald Dore (1983) and Mark Granovetter (1985) describe this, Dore for companies in Britain and Japan, Granovetter for companies in the United States. Both found that when companies first deal with each other they resemble the economic, commodity-realm ideal. They are rational calculators of their own best advantage who transact with each other at arm's length. If those transactions continue, however, their relationship becomes less adversarial and more concerned with fairness and mutual obligation, a decreasing willingness to take advantage and an increasing concern for mutuality and cooperation. This appears to apply even to firms in the financial sector in the twenty-first century, as indicated by a comment by a member of a firm that was worried about the actions of Barclays Bank: "We have been a longtime client of Barclays, which comes with its own responsibilities for Barclays" (quoted in Stewart 2017).

This is not an example of Sahlins's assertion that gifts make friends, for the transactions are not gifts and the relationship is not friendship, but it suggests something similar: that transactions make obligations. It would seem, then, that those firms that come to have obligations to each other are not simply deviating from the dictates of economistic logic. They may be deviating, but that deviation reflects a social logic of its own – the sort that interests economic anthropologists.

This is the sort of logic that is an aspect of what is called "moral economy" (Carrier 2018b). Work on the topic draws especially on E. P. Thompson's (1971) analysis of food riots in rural England around 1800 and James C. Scott's (1976) analysis of peasant uprisings in Southeast Asia around 1900. They argued that long-established forms of transaction among sets of people brought with them ideas of what those different sets owed to each other. In different ways, these moral obligations were displaced by encroaching liberal market systems. These knew nothing of those obligations and led to the unrest that Thompson and Scott describe.

Property and possession

I have said that in commodity systems objects are impersonal, fungible bundles of use and exchange value. They are associated with people, but this is an impersonal association: that of being property in the formal sense. Property is a legal relationship between person and thing, and within broad limits any person can own any thing. In addition, and again within broad limits, owners can use their property, destroy it, sell it, give it away – whatever they like. In gift systems the association between person and thing is that of possession, which is a personal relationship that may have no legal standing and may, in fact, exist only in that person's mind, however, because possession echoes a cultural category, it may exist in many people's minds rather than just the possessor's.

For most of us, an object becomes our property when we purchase it, and, although we are unlikely to think of it that way, the purchase is a legal arrangement in which the seller transfers ownership of the property to the buyer in return for a consideration, the purchase price. This is true even of paid employment, although that is hedged about with legal constraints. Whether there is a written contract or not, the person who is employed transfers to the employer control over what the employee will do for a consideration: the pay. The employee is, in effect, transferring to the employer the ownership of his or her labour power, the ability to labour, for the working day. How the employer can dispose of that labour power is more restricted than how I can dispose of a pair of socks that I bought, but within those restrictions the form of ownership is the same.

This is different from how an object becomes a possession. One way that it can do so is when a person makes it, however, as I described of historical changes in production, not all making is alike. The more that people exercise their discretion in the making, which also means the more that they control it, the more likely the things that they produce are not only expressions of themselves but also are their possessions. The person who chooses to bake a cake from scratch turns impersonal and fungible commodities such as flour, salt, eggs and milk into something that is clearly a possession, while those who work on an automobile assembly line putting hubcaps on every wheel that presents itself at their station do not turn impersonal commodities into possessions but into someone else's property.

Property and possession are not just theoretical concepts. In addition, as stated, they are likely to be part of the cultural understanding of things. The home-made cake looks home-made and personal, and so signals that it is a possession. The automobile in the showroom looks like an impersonal factory product, and so signals that it is only property. Because impersonal property and personal possession are part of cultural understanding, they can be manipulated in ways that depart from the theoretical distinction. Consider the uniform sliced loaf of bread in a plastic bag on a supermarket shelf and the uneven, unsliced loaf of bread in the display case in the neighbourhood bakery. In theoretical terms both are commodities that are property, available for sale to anyone who has the money. Culturally, however, the supermarket loaf looks like property. Conversely, even though people may in fact know nothing about how it was produced, the bakery loaf looks like a possession, hand-made by a careful baker who is, no doubt, an artisan.

In cultural terms, then, there are techniques for moving something from property to possession and back again. In theoretical terms these are processes of appropriation and alienation, and people do both all the time.

Alienation has interested political economists more than economic anthropologists, and they have seen it mostly in fairly impersonal and systemic terms. Those are the sorts of terms that I have used to describe modern factory production, particularly the separation of the conception and execution of work in the Ford Highland Park plant. This approach is descended from Marx's work on the rise of industrial capitalism and paid labour, the proletariat. Members of the proletariat sell their labour power to capitalist employers, and work at the direction of those employers using tools and equipment owned by their employers to make products that belong to the employers. In all this, workers are alienated from the things that they make, but the analytical approach is focused on systems and classes of people considered in fairly abstract terms. This is different from economic anthropologists, who are also concerned with more personal processes, understandings and activities.

Anthropologists commonly see alienation not as a state but as a process, one that occurs when things that had been possessions are lost to the possessor. People confront this loss routinely, whenever they throw out something that they had possessed. Many of those things are mundane to the point of being insignificant: egg shells, used paper, worn-out socks. Although this throwing out fits the definition of alienation, the fact that it is routine and insignificant means that it attracts little academic or public attention. Other sorts of throwing out are more interesting, although they have not attracted much more interest.

These sorts cause people more trouble, and one way that they deal with it is not to do it. Often people keep the bit of coral they brought home as a souvenir from their first trip to the Caribbean, the clay dish that their son produced when he was in the second grade or even the old scarf that they bought ten years ago and have got used to. My father died in 1981. The only remaining thing of his that I have is his wristwatch, which he bought in the 1940s. It no longer works and I do not think that it can be repaired. Even so, I do not want to throw it out.

The result is a lot of clutter in people's lives. Getting rid of the clutter, as people such as Marie Kondo (e.g. 2014) urge, may make our rooms more tidy and plain, and so better-looking. If the clutter is mementos, however, what people are doing is alienating possessions, discarding parts of their past and the people and relationships associated with them. This seems to be difficult. If it were easy, people would not buy books that justify it and tell them how to do it, nor would they write newspaper columns about it.

Fernanda Santos wrote such a column in 2019, and *The New York Times* thought it important enough to publish it (Santos 2019). When Santos's husband died she confronted a bedroom closet full of his clothes, which were part of his life and his relationship with her, and hence part of her life. She realized that she should dispose of them, but could not simply throw them out. After more than a year she selected a charity that espoused values that were important to her husband. She donated the clothes to them.

There are more conventional ways of alienating possessions that do not lead to op-ed pieces in national newspapers. A common one is called a car boot sale in the United Kingdom, a garage sale or lawn sale in the United States. In these, people get rid of things for money, and do so in a particular way. These are fairly social events and, especially in the United States, attract neighbours, so that the alienation does not seem as absolute as it would if the items were sold to impersonal dealers in used clothing and furniture. This sociality of objects appears in a different form in another sort of yard sale, one in which a woman announces that she is getting rid of the things that her ex left behind when he abandoned her and moved out or when she threw him out. Here the alienation is a renunciation, necessary because the things for sale are possessions. In publicly ejecting them from her home the woman publicly ejects the man associated with them and the relationship that she had with him.

Anthropologists have more to say about appropriation, making something a possession, because they have long been interested in how people make and give things. As I have said, the more that people control the making of something the more it is likely to be an expression of their interests and abilities and so be a possession of the makers. Equally, as noted in this chapter, the more that people give and receive things in durable social relations, the more they are likely to be possessions. In the markets that characterize commodity systems, however, people are likely to confront a lot of things that they neither make nor give, and so have to work to appropriate them in some way.

One way that they do so is by modifying the thing, which puts their mark on it and makes it more personal. For instance, chefs who take their work seriously season dishes the way that they think that they ought to be, so that the customer is presented with something complete. Probably without thinking about it, those customers routinely sprinkle salt and pepper on the food, modifying it so that it bears to some degree their preferences and practices, and hence their personality, rather than solely that of the chef. Similarly, people break things in, stamp them with their identity. In the process they use them, which makes them become familiar, and often modify them in minor ways. Daniel Miller (1988) describes how people stamp their identity on their council housing in London – that is, housing owned by the local government and allocated to those who qualify for it because of their income. He found that the tenants who were most comfortable with their housing were those who had marked it in some way with minor decorations, the only sort that council regulations allowed. In other words, they had appropriated their living space to make it more their own. In the words of his title, they were "appropriating the state on the council estate".

Another and less obvious way that people appropriate things is by selection. Confronted with a range of options in a supermarket aisle, people select some things rather than others. This is especially important with foodstuffs, which people take home and turn into a meal to be eaten, alone or in company. Again, Miller's (1998) work is interesting, this time his study of people in north London as they did their shopping.

He found that people approached things not simply in terms of what those things were, such as a tin of tomatoes, but also in terms of how they would be used, an ingredient in spaghetti sauce. Further, the use that concerned them was not private – a meal that the shopper liked – but social: a meal that the shopper would share with someone else, such as family, flat-mate, friends, partner. Poignantly, he found that those who lived and dined alone occasionally would speak of others with whom they had shared meals in the past or with whom they hoped to share in the future. Miller's work indicates that ordinary shopping is not simply acquiring utilities in return for money, the sort of activity that shows up in economic statistics. In addition, it is turning indifferent commodities into elements in social relations, turning property into possession.

A different form of selection also helps people appropriate commodities: the selection that comes from careful shopping for the best deal. This is likely to result in shoppers getting more for their money, although we cannot be sure of this until we defetishize the purchases. In this case that would mean taking into account the time, effort and money that careful shoppers spend to find out what the best deals are and where they are and making their purchases. We can be sure, however, that careful shopping turns purchasing into the shopper's work, and so helps that shopper appropriate what is bought. These tins of tomatoes and that dozen eggs are not the random effects of going out to buy. Rather, they are the result of intentional effort that is guided by the shopper's desires and so marks them with the shopper's identity.

The appropriation that I have described is a way that people try to make sure that the objects in their lives are suited to the social relations in which they will exist. The need to appropriate those objects varies as people's experience with and understanding of their nature changes. In an earlier chapter I described a change in that nature as the organization and relations of production changed. The nature of objects changes as well when common forms of circulation change. I turn to that in the next chapter.

5

Commercial circulation

I have said that economic anthropology provides a perspective that helps us to see familiar things in new ways. One example of this is the description of historical changes in production in an earlier chapter. People commonly see those changes in terms of technological advance and improved efficiency. Those things are real, but the anthropology encourages us to see how they are related to other areas of people's lives, particularly their social relations and understandings of their world.

Two aspects of that history are important. One is that the relations in which production took place increasingly were impersonal, as those who did the work became more alienated from their colleagues and from what they were doing. The other is that workers were less and less likely actually to make anything and so were less likely to know how things are made. The household that wove the cloth undertook most of the steps involved; the worker on a moving assembly line undertook only a small part of the production of an automobile. Not all production changed in this way, but enough did that it affected common understandings of production and of objects produced.

Such changes occurred as well in the way that people transacted objects in commercial circulation, buying and selling. This chapter complements that history of production, for here I trace changes in the nature of commercial circulation up to the point where the modern retail market became pervasive, which was in the first half of the twentieth century. These changes show that people bought more and more of what they needed rather than making it, and did so in settings that were increasingly impersonal. These changes appeared first in large cities. The one that I shall focus on is London, although similar changes appeared at about the same time in Amsterdam and Paris. Gradually they came to pervade buying and selling pretty much everywhere, and I shall describe changes elsewhere in the United Kingdom and in the United States. To understand the significance of these changes it is necessary to understand what went before, and I begin with how things were in England.

The old order

Before the eighteenth century the situation and orientation of most people in England resembled the Colombian peasants and their house economy, described in a previous chapter. Like those Colombians, English households were not wholly self-sufficient, and they acquired in trade the things that they did not produce. That trade was not simply a consequence of objective economic factors but also reflected the linked values of self-sufficiency and localism. They were present everywhere in the country but were especially important in rural areas, which is where the vast majority of English people lived. According to Peter Borsay (1989: 3), at the beginning of the eighteenth century England had only around 70 villages and towns of over 2,500 inhabitants and just three cities of over 20,000, one of which was London, with a population of half a million.

Transport was adequate to allow people to travel to fairly distant places to buy and sell, but few of them did so. Rather, the bulk of their trading took place in market towns. These were sufficiently widespread that most people, even in rural areas, could go to one, do their business and come back in less than a day. For most English people, then, the nearby market town was as far as they went to buy and sell, and their sense of commercial transaction and of the objects transacted was shaped by their experience of market trade, as was the case for most of English-speaking North America as well.

Localism and self-sufficiency were enshrined in law as well as in people's values. Hoping to reduce the chance of widespread unrest in times of dearth, government bodies sought to ensure that local produce went to local people. For instance, market authorities required those who sold in the market to pay a toll, and what they charged to outside traders often was twice what they charged to locals. Further, outsiders who were not established traders were likely to be taken up as vagrants and expelled from the parish, the unit of local administration. In addition, market regulations routinely required sellers to offer their produce to local householders before they could sell to anyone else. Even in urban markets the first hour or two of trading commonly was restricted to sales to local householders, as traders and shopkeepers were excluded.

This orientation was reinforced by a general distrust of pure merchants, those who bought only in order to sell. Rather, the belief was that goods should pass direct from producer to consumer. One pamphlet early in the nineteenth century said of pure merchants that "their meer *handing of Goods one to another*, no more increases any Wealth in the Province, then Persons *at a Fire* increase the *Water in a Pail*, by passing it thro' Twenty or Forty hands" (quoted in Crowley 1974: 88, emphasis in original). Accordingly, people generally were allowed to sell what they had bought only if they had transformed it in some way. For instance, bakers could sell the flour and meal that they had bought only after they had turned it into bread; ironmongers could sell their metal only after they had turned it into rakes, keys and hinges.

Markets had formal governing authorities, but the main institution that enforced these values and practices was the open market. What I said above indicates that it was not open in the sense that it was free for all. Rather, it was open in the sense that transactions were visible to all. Private dealing in inns or people's homes was prohibited, as was buying a farmer's crop or a fisher's catch directly from the producer before it was offered in the market, a practice called forestalling. Having transactions be visible in this way allowed people to see what things such as the flour and meal cost. It was also intended to protect buyers and sellers from sharp practice and deception, and the definition of sharp practice was broad, including trading in order to gain at another person's expense.

These regulations were not effective everywhere and not everyone bought and sold in this way. For most people in England, however, localism meant that when they bought or sold they did so with people whom they knew, with whom they transacted repeatedly and with whom they shared understandings of how transactors ought to act. In rural areas often they did transact, rather than only buy or sell. The accounts of a village shop in the 1780s in Didsbury, near what is now the English city of Manchester, showed not only the value of items that customers bought from the shopkeeper but also the value of the services that they performed for him, such as cutting hay and getting rid of molehills (Mui & Mui 1989: 40). In rural areas in the United States well into the nineteenth century these sorts of transactions also were common. Gerald Carson describes it:

In the ledger the customer who received goods on tick was marked debtor. [...] Frequently there would be an entry in both [debt and credit] columns, the buyer of merchandise receiving credit for live chickens or shoeing the storekeeper's horse. The accounts were continuous, and settlement infrequent, though the almanacs advised settlement annually, around December or January. (Carson 1954: 97–8)

This was not, then, the anonymity of the shopper and the supermarket checkout assistant but give-and-take that linked people to each other, each transaction building on previous ones and laying the foundation for future ones.

Familiarity between buyers and sellers was not restricted to local merchants, but was important also for long-distance trade, trade beyond the locality, although it usually had a different basis. It mostly relied on kin links, which offered a degree of security for those involved. Alan Everitt describes how a

group of Thanet farmers who sent malt to the capital in James I's reign were not only themselves related, but operated through London factors who were their own nephews and cousins. [...] [Likewise, the] purchase of Kentish fruit by London fruiterers, and their ownership of orchards in the countryside around Teynham, often arose from their intermarriage with the daughters of Kentish farmers and from the fact that they were themselves sons or cousins of Kentish yeomen. (Everitt 1967: 513)

Such links remained important in central areas of manufacturing and trade in England into the nineteenth century, notably among Quakers (Davidoff & Hall 1987: 215–22), as they remain important everywhere in the present among those who transact expensive things, especially if they are difficult to value, such as uncut diamonds.

I have described local market trade in England because there was relatively little of what we would call pure retail trade. In that, a merchant buys things in order to offer them for sale in a shop, which would violate the rule that those who bought things had to transform them before they could sell them. There were early shops, but rarely were they purely retail. Rather, most shops were run by artisans who sold from the front room of their house the things that they had made in the back room, while they lived in the upper storeys. As this suggests, shops did not look different from ordinary houses, although they might have a window somewhat larger than usual. That was called a "vent" and was where transactions took place.

Some shops did sell things that were not made locally, and so did not transform them in the way that a brewer turned barley into beer. Tea and coffee were obvious examples, as were dried fruits and a range of other products. Even though they may not have transformed these things as much as did brewers and bakers, shopkeepers routinely worked on what they had bought before selling it: they blended teas, sweetened wines, graded and sorted raisins, finished cloths, and so on. This was not the only way that their wares were stamped with the shopkeeper's identity, so that they were not simply impersonal commodities.

For one thing, shopkeeping was not simply a job. Instead, it was a trade in which people were trained in apprenticeships, in which they learned not just the technical aspects of the trade but also the customs, practices and values associated with it. The result was that the successful apprentice was likely to identify personally with the trade, so that carrying it out became an expression of the shopkeeper's identity. For another, whether artisans or not, all shopkeepers had to buy things, whether stocks of tea to blend or leather to turn into shoes. So, they needed suppliers.

Suppliers would not deal with just any shopkeeper, however, in the same way that shopkeepers would not deal with just any supplier. Each needed to trust the other, personally in terms of their honesty and professionally in terms of their knowledge of the quality of their wares and their knowledge of their trade. Not least this was because the shopkeeper who bought stock or raw materials commonly needed a substantial amount of credit extended over a significant amount of time. So, shopkeepers and suppliers had to get to know and trust each other, and one thing that apprentices acquired was knowledge of different suppliers, just as they became known to those suppliers. As a result, their dealings ended up being as much social as they were economic, a sociality that shaped the nature of what shopkeepers acquired.

Shopkeepers and artisans commonly lived above the shop, but the conjunction of home and shop was conceptual as well as spatial. Shopkeepers rarely saw their businesses as what Stephen Gudeman and Alberto Rivera (1991) call a corporation, a separate commercial entity that the shopkeeper happened to own. Rather, shop and household blended into each other. Family members worked in the shop as needed and shop workers, usually apprentices, worked in the household as needed. Expenses for each often were charged to the other. Apprentices were treated as household members, just as the children in the household often were apprenticed to the person who headed the household and the shop. Customers at a shop, then, were not buying impersonal objects from paid employees who would go home at the end of the day. Rather, they were likely to be in household space dealing with household members and acquiring things that were in some measure household products.

Relations between customers and shopkeepers were likely to be fairly social for another reason as well. Shops of all sorts were fairly small and had a fairly small number of customers, so that shopkeeper and customer were likely to get to know each other. A British government survey of 1759, which is likely to have undercounted small shops, found that in southern England there were only 35.3 residents per shop, while in London there were fewer, 30 (Mui & Mui 1989: 40). In many areas, in fact, shops commonly were what the government called "inward rooms" – shops with no separate entrance. In other words, customers had to go through the shopkeeper's household space in order to reach the selling space.

Drawing on Polanyi's *The Great Transformation* (1944), anthropologists say that this sort of economic activity is "embedded". This means that it is carried out among those who are linked by social relationships, not simply by economic ones – relationships that provide a framework of moral expectation for transactors. When more impersonal economistic thought and practice spread, which is what Polanyi described in his book, the obligations that transactors had toward each other were weakened or even denied.

In *The Wealth of Nations* Adam Smith expressed, and advocated, economistic thought when he said that there were only two possible motives for economic transaction, charity and self-interest, ruling out obligation. As he (1976 [1776]: 18) put it, "It is not from the benevolence of the butcher, the brewer, or the baker, that we expect our dinner, but from their regard to their own interest." The result is that, in our dealings with our fellows, "[w]e address ourselves, not to their humanity, but to their self-love, and never talk to them of our own necessities, but of their advantages". In significant parts of rural England, the growing denial of the older economic order and its attendant obligations late in the eighteenth century was met by civil unrest of the sort that E. P. Thompson (1971) describes.

This embedded economy meant that, for most people, most of the objects in their lives were either things that they had produced or things acquired in transactions between those in fairly durable social relations. In C. A. Gregory's terms, then, they were acquired through transactions in something like gift relationships and so were possessions rather than impersonal commodities.

This embedding, this importance of social relations in economic life, had its disadvantages. Poorer customers regularly needed credit, and could find themselves becoming dependent on shopkeepers who offered it. Conversely, shopkeepers could become dependent on richer customers, who might run up large debts and be slow to pay them off. Disembedding, which occurred in many parts of economic life in the century after Smith wrote, helped to free people from these dependencies.

Disembedding

The system of embedded commerce weakened significantly from late in the eighteenth century, most quickly in urban areas. Like Smith, a growing number of people advocated a more impersonal view of commerce closer to our own and closer to the conventional economistic approach. Disembedded retail trade grew especially in London in the decades around 1800, but even there changes were more apparent in richer areas of the city and in some branches of trade than they were in others.

One thing encouraging this was changes in production in the second half of the eighteenth century. Factories were becoming more common, leading to higher levels of output and to products that were more uniform, and so easier for the purchaser to assess independently. In addition, more factories meant more female and child labour, so that households had fewer people to do the conventional subsistence activities of making and mending. Instead, they had to buy more of what they needed, and to get the money they had to devote more time to wage labour, a process that became self-sustaining (a point I return to in a later chapter). Even in rural areas the enclosing of what had been common land meant that households had to buy more to replace what they could no longer produce for themselves on the commons, and those who could not generate the money migrated to town for work. This growth in demand, together with the growing urban population in England, meant that the ideal of localism went to the wall, as did the belief that people should not buy solely in order to resell. Intermediaries became common, though hardly universal even in London, so that the circulation of things became less visible and people's experience of commercial circulation began to change.

Retail trade increased most visibly for things that previously had been traded little, such as the clothing that most ordinary households previously had produced for themselves as part of their making and mending. The consequence was that new people entered retail trade and new approaches emerged. The significance of these changes is attested by the fact that from around 1790 to 1810 several retail firms catering to the better off opened in London that remained important into the last quarter of the twentieth century.

For our purposes, however, what is important is that a growing number of shopkeepers were changing their views of what we would call consumer demand, away from an established body of customers with whom they were enmeshed in a set of mutual obligations of a greater or lesser weight. Instead, they came to think in terms of an impersonal mass with whom they sought to trade with regard to what Smith stressed: their own interest. This meant something like a separation of shopkeepers from customers, and this disembedding of their economic relationship had different effects at different levels. At the upper level, shopkeepers began to band together to end their dependence on powerful, rich customers. At the lower level, poorer customers began to band together to demand better treatment from shopkeepers. The disembedding had a material corollary, as shop and household became more distinct and shopkeepers began to commute to work, although in 1800 this was common only in wealthy areas of London.

The changing orientation toward an impersonal market was manifest in growing attention to what was called the "dropping trade": strangers who passed by the shop and dropped in to buy. One consequence was the spread of large window displays – part of the growing difference in appearance between shops and residences. This began in fashionable parts of London late in the eighteenth century and gradually spread. Henry Mayhew, a journalist and social commentator in London around the middle of the nineteenth century, summarized the difference between old and new shop fronts and the attitudes that went with them:

> The quiet house of the honourable tailor, with the name inscribed on the window blinds, or on the brass-plate on the door, tells you that the proprietor has no wish to compete with or undersell his neighbour. But at the show and slop-shops every art and trick that scheming can devise or avarice suggest, is displayed to attract the notice of the passer-by, and filch the customer from another. The quiet, unobtrusive place of business of the old-fashioned tailor is transformed into the flashy palace of the grasping tradesman.
>
> (Mayhew 1849)

Orientation toward an anonymous and impersonal market also appeared in new pricing practices. One of these was fixed pricing, which meant that the shopkeeper would not vary the price first quoted to the shopper. This eliminated haggling, which made the buying transaction more mechanical and the work of sales staff more impersonal and less discretionary. More important was open ticketing, which meant that the price was plainly visible to potential buyers, although to complicate matters this may have been only the first or highest price, not the lower price offered to favoured customers. Whatever the practicalities and complexities of fixed pricing and open ticketing, by around 1800 London shops were announcing that they sold goods for cash at fixed prices. This was the foundation of the price competition between shopkeepers that Mayhew mentioned, which weakened the social cohesion of those in retail trade.

This also marked the decreasing place of credit in retail trade, which had linked shopkeepers and customers. Hitherto, credit had been an expected part of trade at every level. The rich saw credit as a matter of routine, and the shops that dealt with them sent out statements once or twice a year, so that customers may not have known what their purchases cost until the account arrived months later. The poor needed credit because of economic uncertainty. Jobs were unstable and pay was uncertain, and there was always the risk of illness, leading to a loss of earnings, or the cost of important social events such as weddings and funerals.

Although credit was a convenience for the rich it was a necessity for the poor, and it took time to become known to local merchants well enough that they would extend credit. Credit was so important and it took so long to become known to local shopkeepers that the inability to transfer a good reputation from one area to another appears to have been an important factor restricting the geographic mobility of the working class in England as late as the start of the twentieth century (Jones 1971: 88).

Shops advertising fixed prices for ready money to an anonymous public became noticeable in London in the 1780s and called themselves warehouses to imply that their prices were low. This was especially so in the growing trade in clothing aimed at the lower layers of the middle class. Such shops sought a high volume of trade and advertised heavily to attract anonymous buyers. Again, Mayhew (1849, emphasis in original) described this: "Every article in the window is ticketed – the price is cut down *to the quick* – books of crude, bold verse are thrust in your hands, or thrown into your carriage window – the panels of every omnibus are plastered with show placards, telling you how Messrs —— defy competition."

Growing attention to the dropping trade and the spread of shops aimed at a high volume of trade also further undercut the idea of the open market. The villager who bought bread from the local baker knew what the baker was paying for flour, because it was bought in the open market. The show and slop shops that Mayhew mentioned were buying stock in transactions that were not generally visible, however. Transactions other than purchases that people made themselves were becoming opaque, and their ability to assess the commercial position of the shops where they made them was disappearing.

Also around 1800 some manufacturers began to advertise their products along with their prices, although it was only in the second half of the nineteenth century that branded goods and national advertising spread. As branded goods became more common and entered popular thought, the position of shopkeepers changed in another way. Instead of establishing relations with suppliers who offered at a reasonable price goods that the shopkeeper thought that his customers would like, shopkeepers increasingly were passive, caught between large manufacturers and the demand that their advertisements generated. What the shopkeeper or assistant knew of the quality of different products was irrelevant to the customer who came in and demanded a tin of Heinz beans, especially one who had been warned by the manufacturer against deceitful assistants who might try to fob them off with something else.

Institutional changes

The changing ways that shops dealt with customers made buying more impersonal, so that what people bought began to resemble commodities, both in Gregory's sense and in the sense of anonymous manufactures. Changes in the organization and operation of retail firms had the same effect, even if they were less visible to shoppers. Like the changes already described, these changes affected different regions and different branches of trade in different ways and at different times.

I said that the increasing orientation to the dropping trade made it less likely that shop staff and customers would become familiar with each other. One institutional change reduced that likelihood even further: the appearance of larger stores designed to deal with more customers. Aside from the warehouses and monster shops, most establishments that were purely retail were small, perhaps 20 to 40 feet (6 to 12 m) deep and 10 to 15 feet (3 to 4.5 m) wide. This was not all open space, for it included a storage room in the back, shelves and cupboards filled with goods, the counter over which customers and shop staff faced each other, the shopkeeper, perhaps an assistant and, of course, customers themselves. An example, from fairly late in the nineteenth century, is F. W. Woolworth's in the United States (Woolworth 1954). The company opened three stores in the firm's first year, 1879. The average size was 360 square feet (33.5 m²) and the largest of the three was 14 × 35 feet (4.3 × 10.7 m).

This was a far cry from the Thomas Lipton Company, which opened stores in different parts of Scotland late in the 1870s. The Dundee store had 12 to 15 assistants and three cash boys, the Paisley store had a counter served by 12 assistants and the main Glasgow store could hold 200 customers and had a counter that was 100 feet (30 m) long (Mathias 1967: 46). Larger shops with more customers and transactions meant that impersonality was becoming a necessity rather than a choice.

At around the same time the scope of stores increased because of the emergence of chain (in the United States) or multiple (in the United Kingdom) stores. In both countries these sorts of stores expanded and so increased the proportion of the population that experienced them as they acquired objects. In the United States late in the 1920s chain stores account for just under a tenth of all retail trade; in Britain around 1915 they accounted for about the same. The spread of these chains marked a further step in something that I have mentioned already: the invisibility of the commercial transactions in which retailers bought what they sold to customers.

Some of the new chains and multiples sought to take advantage of a new market, the working class, which was becoming important around 1900 as workers' position improved. They did not have their branch stores in middle-class parts of cities but in industrial areas, and their stores carried a limited line of staple foodstuffs and household goods and emphasized low prices. An example in the United States is A&P (Great Atlantic and Pacific Tea Company) stores. In the 1880s they sold only tea, coffee, sugar, spices, butter and condensed milk (Walsh 1986: 22–3). In the United Kingdom Maypole Dairy had about 800 branches, and in 1913 it sold only eggs, condensed milk, tea, margarine and butter. In 1914 it stopped selling eggs (Mathias 1967: 173). With these stores, impersonal trade spread to the lower classes.

These chains and multiples used centralized procedures that tended to alienate staff from the store itself, their customers and even their trade. Most obviously, store managers were not owners; what they stocked was dictated and supplied by their employer, and their loyalty was supposed to be directed to the firm rather than to the store; many companies regularly moved managers to different stores to encourage this. Additionally, company policies constrained managers in a variety of ways, reducing the degree to which the store and what went on in it was an expression of the manager. In fact, firms wanted this alienation. They saw the older-style shopkeepers, brought up in the trade and identifying with it, bound to their area and their customers, as backward-looking and unable to move with the increasingly rational and profit-oriented times. According to William Walsh (1986: 30), early in the twentieth century the A&P chain decided to hire as managers only those with no retail experience, because they had "no built-in bad retail habits" to unlearn.

The same applied to store assistants, who increasingly were the only people customers dealt with. Commonly they had been apprentices who were learning a trade and had prospects of having shops of their own.

Increasingly they were wage workers without skills, and unlikely to learn any; employees of the firm that hired them, but not part of it and with no prospects of advancement. And, as with branch managers, many companies preferred to hire such people. One observer of American supermarkets in the 1930s summarized companies' viewpoint thus:

> All our help is composed of young men and boys … We can train a man on stock in an hour – on cashiering, in a few days. We can start with an entire new crew and operate very efficiently even to having one of them make out the orders. The less they know about the grocery business, the better. We have and want a large turnover in regular help because the work is monotonous and hard and as the boys develop, we place them in new markets. Better positions of course are not many. This is a condition that we recognize as not being conducive to building a loyal organization because of limitations in advancement.
> (Zimmerman 1937: 107)

These sorts of managerial orientation spread in retail trade, and people bought more and more in such stores. The result was that a growing proportion of people's commercial transactions, their buying and selling, occurred in institutional settings that resembled Ford's Highland Park assembly lines. The shop assistants may have been sociable but, as I noted in a previous chapter, that was part of their job. And that sociability was different from the personality and obligation that was important in the older trade. It should not, then, be surprising that, early in the twentieth century, William Allen White, an American defender of the old order, complained about the new: "There is such a thing as 'tainted' dry goods, 'tainted' groceries and 'tainted' furniture … All of such that are not bought at home, of men who befriended you, of men to whom you owe a living, are 'tainted' because they come unfairly" (quoted in Strasser 1989: 216).

I have ended this history in the first half of the twentieth century. Since then retail trade and people's experience have changed, most visibly with the appearance of self-service checkout at supermarkets, the rise of online buying and centralized retailers such as Amazon, the extension of retail chains and their consolidation through mergers. These changes have important consequences, and any walk through a commercial area of town will reveal some of them. But generally they have meant only the further reduction of any human contact in buying and selling and the reinforcing of the impersonality of circulation.

One further extension of these changes merits attention. It is the invisibility of commercial transactions other than those in which one is involved directly. As I noted, how a supermarket chain gets its tins of beans and bottles of milk is invisible in practice. In the closing decades of the twentieth century, however, it became invisible in principle as well. Attempts to make those things visible came to be rejected with the statement that commercial confidentiality means that they are secret. Thus, in 2019 a number of hospital chains in the United States went to court to block the implementation of a federal rule that would require them to disclose how much they pay their suppliers for various medical objects and services (Abelson 2019). Even governments in the United States and the United Kingdom, responsible to their citizenry, invoke commercial confidentiality to keep secret how much they pay commercial firms to carry out various government works. So, it is not just human content in buying and selling that has disappeared. The open market has disappeared as well.

In the end, customers may have liked the changes in commercial circulation that I have described, just as they may have liked what came off the line at Highland Park, although by the middle of the twentieth century few people in the United States and the United Kingdom had enough experience with anything else to allow them to make a comparison. Happy or not, these changes in the ways that people transacted objects had consequences, and in the next chapter I turn to an important one.

6

Considering Christmas

I have described some of the important analytical models that economic anthropologists use when they approach production and circulation, as well as historical changes in these two realms of economic life, especially in the United States and the United Kingdom. Now I want to show the kinds of insights that the models and histories can provide by using them to address something that those who read this book are likely to see as familiar: Christmas.

In the United States and the United Kingdom, Christmas is a holiday. The 25th of December is a holy day marked on the church calendar of western Christian denominations, and many believers observe it with special services and ceremonies. But Christmas is also a civic holiday, one that those of any or no religion are likely to observe as well, but in a different sense. They are likely to observe it in the shops as the Christmas displays go up and seasonal items appear on the shelves. They observe it in the office parties and family gatherings that litter December. They observe it on radio and television, as Christmas music and movies appear. Even the online solitaire that I play has a special design for playing cards at Christmas. It is this that makes Christmas a ubiquitous set of activities and experiences in these countries, and it is this civic event that concerns me in this chapter. I want to make that familiar event seem strange by making use of those analytical models and historical changes.

If you think about it, Christmas is full of contradictions for those who experience it. People tell each other that it is a festive season of good cheer, but, equally, they say that the fun is going out of it, swamped by materialism and commerce. Christmas goods seem to appear in the stores earlier every year, as do the advertisements on television telling us to buy more and more things for more and more people. This slights the religious beliefs that many see as an important part of Christmas and conflicts with religious reservations about wealth and its display. In spite of people's concern with the garish commercialization, the stores get more crowded and the websites get slower. Feeling frazzled with all the shopping, people tell themselves that they will be more organized next year – just as they told themselves the same thing last year.

Like those plans to be more organized next year, the complaints about the rush, the crush and the spending are not new. Late in the 1980s a columnist in *The Washington Post*, William Raspberry (1988), put his complaint in a piece entitled "Christmas run amok: our gift-giving has gotten out of hand". Almost 30 years before that the singer Tom Lehrer (1959) released "A Christmas carol", satirizing the commercialization of Christmas. About 20 years earlier many Americans complained that money was overwhelming spiritual values when President Roosevelt moved Thanksgiving Day a week earlier, to encourage more Christmas commerce. Thirty years before that *The Times* complained about the commercialization of Christmas in the United Kingdom, and 20 years earlier still *The Ladies' Home Journal* complained about the same thing in the United States.

If commercialization has been taking over Christmas and the fun has been going out of it for well over a century, why do people who keep complaining about it keep doing it? If people want to keep the season and avoid the commercial misery, why not simply send people cards or just wish them a merry Christmas, perhaps throwing in an affectionate expression such as "My dear"? Understanding why people keep doing it and complaining about it while they do so requires picking apart the Christmas season and seeing why and how it makes sense to so many people, even those who have never been to a Christmas Eve church service in their lives.

Christmas giving

The Christmas season is a time of intense circulation, as people shop for objects, food and drink that they will circulate as presents, meals and parties. This circulation is the core of the season, and it is widespread, with office parties and presents to school classmates and donations to charities. It has a focus, however, which is a loving couple and their children, the affectionate core of the nuclear family.

To say that this is a cultural focus is to say that it is a story that we tell ourselves about the spirit of the season, even if our actual lives are different. Couples without children or whose family relations are badly frayed recognize it, perhaps with sadness or bitterness, as do those who live alone. That recognition is reinforced by the images in advertisements aimed at Christmas shoppers and in different ways by seasonal romantic comedies, such as the classics *Miracle on 34th Street* (Twentieth Century Fox 1947), set in the United States, and *Love Actually* (Universal Pictures 2003), set in the United Kingdom, and such as the new ones that are released every year. They show that, even for those who are alone at the start of the season, this is the time when love triumphs. And not just love, but marriage: it seems that Christmas and Christmas Eve are the two most popular days to propose marriage in the United States (Frost 2018).

This is not just any love. It is affectionate, familial love, the sort that comes with hearth and home, and in the United States and the United Kingdom hearth and home culturally remain the domain primarily of women. Accordingly, much of Christmas is seen as women's work. They normally are the ones who wrap the presents, decide who ought to be invited to Christmas dinner and prepare the meal, the most important one in the year in the United Kingdom and second only to Thanksgiving in the United States. They are the ones who normally send out the cards, and, even if they do not do all the Christmas shopping, it is assumed that they will make sure that it is done. This does not mean that all women do all this work, and do it just because they are women. Differences in individual temperament and interest, as well as the history of individual relations and situations in families, can lead to different tasks being carried out by different household members. The reality of these differences does not, however, rebut the point that Christmas is not just a family celebration, it is a celebration of the familial; and that, culturally, the family realm is feminine.

This focus on the affectionate family is echoed in Christmas giving. In the United States and the United Kingdom gifts within the immediate family, couples and their children, account for the vast majority of the largest single presents that people give and for the bulk of the money that most people spend on presents. In addition, it is in family giving that givers have the least concern for the cost of the gifts given and the value of the gifts received, being concerned instead that the gift reflects the giver, the recipient and their close relationship. As we move away from this, giving changes, even gifts to kin. Giving to siblings and collaterals is more dependent on whether or not they live near the giver, and, in this giving, as I noted in a previous chapter, people are more concerned that gifts given and received are of approximately equal value. This pattern in the ways that people transact with each other resembles Marshall Sahlins's description of generalized and balanced reciprocity.

When we move beyond home and kin, to things such as gifts in the office, the giving is more formulaic and less personal. Gifts from bosses to secretaries are fairly standard, and in December chocolate shops sell a lot of boxes with the appropriate assortment and the appropriate price. Among co-workers there are things such as Secret Santa, an example of giving that looks almost as though the people who thought it up had read Sahlins on balanced reciprocity. In it, people go out and buy gifts that cost the amount announced in advance, bring them to the office on the day, pull each other's names out of a hat and hand the gift over. More distant yet, gifts to the people who work in your apartment building and deliver your mail and collect your rubbish, like gifts to the people who work in the nursing home where my mother lives, are the least personal thing of all, money, and there is no concern that there be a return gift. Rather than gifts in the conventional sense, these resemble *douceurs*, given in thanks for good service and in the hope that it will continue.

Gifts among that loving couple and their children are a cultural standard, and I have described how other sorts of giving depart from it. In that standard, and especially the loving couple who are the heart of it, we can see in pronounced form a common British and American understanding of the ideal gift given by ideal people in ideal relations. In that understanding the material form and monetary worth of the gift are unimportant, which accounts for the lack of concern with what is key in the *moka*, the value of the return gift. That is because the thing given is only a vehicle for what is central: the link between the gift and the love that the giver has for the recipient. Also in that understanding the gift is freely given, an expression of love that is not constrained in any way. The gift is free in another way as well, for it does not bind the recipient. Equally, because the expression of love is spontaneous it does not bind the giver.

This ideal is expressed in a popular Christmas story from the beginning of the last century, O. Henry's "The gift of the magi" (1917 [1905]). This is a story about a poor, young and loving couple, Jim and Della, living in a

New York flat and considering what to get each other for Christmas. Della decided to sell her long, brown hair, her proudest possession, to a hair-dresser. She did so to get the money to buy a fob chain for Jim's proudest possession, a gold watch that had been passed down from his grandfather to his father and to him. For his part, Jim wanted to buy for Della the tor-toiseshell combs with jewelled rims that she had seen in a store window and longed to have for her hair. To get the money to buy them, he sold his watch.

Jim and Della sacrificed their proudest possessions for love, and, because the hair and watch were gone, each sacrifice was futile. But O. Henry celebrates their love and sacrifice when he ends his story:

> The magi, as you know, were wise men – wonderfully wise men – who brought gifts to the Babe in the manger. They invented the art of giving Christmas presents. Being wise, their gifts were no doubt wise ones, possibly bearing the privilege of exchange in case of duplication. And here I have lamely related to you the uneventful chronicle of two foolish children in a flat who most unwisely sacrificed for each other the greatest treasures of their house. But in a last word to the wise of these days let it be said that of all who give gifts these two were the wisest. Of all who give and receive gifts, such as they are wisest. Everywhere they are wisest. They are the magi. (Henry 1917 [1905]: 25)

In the futile sacrifices that it relates, this story describes the ideal gift. Jim and Della gave up the things that they most valued, but the futility of what they did shows how wrong it is to think of those presents as things. Instead, as Henry relates, those are the best presents that could be: the self given for love. And, because the hair and the watch are each giver's most valued possession, they are equal, so Jim and Della are not beholden to each other.

Jim and Della, their sacrifices and gifts, express an ideal: the notion that, as one commentator put it, "when thinking of the perfect thing to give the person you love, there is no present greater than the gift of your whole life" (Boylan 2019). In more ordinary circumstances more ordinary concerns can be important. Is the gift something that the recipient wants? Does it cost too little, or too much? Is it suited to the occasion and the relationship between giver and recipient? Even in those more ordinary circumstances, however, affectionate giving contains a contradiction. The giving is supposed to be an expression of the heart and of the relationship between giver and recipient, but what people give is a commodity bought in a shop or on a website. Unravelling this contradiction helps show the social forces that shape economic activity at this intense season, forces that lead people to give presents rather than just wishing each other a merry Christmas, with love.

Gifts and commodities once more

Like O. Henry's story, the ideal gift is magical, and to see the magic we need to view the giving with dispassionate eyes that help make it seem strange. Like the combs and the watch fob, the thing that is given is an object of a certain use value and exchange value, almost certainly acquired in a commodity transaction. It is, then, poorly suited to be a personal gift of affection, which should make wishing people a merry Christmas even more attractive.

Recall Emerson's injunction, presented in an earlier chapter, which began "The only gift is a portion of thyself. Thou must bleed for me." He elaborates on "a portion of thyself" when he mentions the poet's poem and the shepherd's lamb. He contrasted things such as this with what is bought when he said that "it is a cold, lifeless business when you go to the shops to buy me something, which does not represent your life and talent, but a goldsmith's" (1983 [1844]: 94). (The things that we buy, of course, seldom represent anything so personal as that.)

The image of the ideal gift, because it is ideal, transcends the contradiction between the impersonality of the purchased object and its use in the loving gift. The notion of the ideal gift is magical because it disembodies the object given, transmutes the dross of its material aspect and exchange value into an expression of love. It is, after all, the thought that counts.

The contradiction that the ideal gift transcends is one that people in less ideal circumstances confront around Christmas: the need to give a personal gift in a world of commodities. They deal with it in an activity described already: appropriating their purchases. One way that they do this is by thinking about presents in a way that makes them special. That is, we say that they should not be simple bundles of utility, however useful they would be. Emerson called those useful gifts "common" and distinguished them from his gifts of compliment and love. He said that, "if the man at the door have no shoes, you have not to consider whether you would procure him a paint-box" (1983 [1844]: 94). Such a gift is something like charity, which the recipient resents: "We wish to be self-sustained. We do not quite forgive a giver" (1983 [1844]: 94). Instead, the Christmas gift should express a relationship, which in practice turns out to mean that it should be luxurious, frivolous or otherwise special in some way.

There is another, material way that people distinguish those gifts from mundane objects of the sort that they transact in the commercial realm or in ordinary circumstances in social relations. They wrap them, which covers the commodity with a layer of festivity and sentiment and makes the giving a prestation. One practice that Theodore Caplow found to be almost universal in Christmas activities in Middletown was wrapping presents, saying that "Christmas gifts must be wrapped before they are presented", although he does say that gifts that are hard to wrap, such as "a pony or a piano, are wrapped symbolically by adding a ribbon or bow or card and hidden until presentation" (Caplow 1984: 1310). To this I would add things such as home-made jam and cake, which are likely to have only a bow. They may be covered in aluminium foil, but that is not seen as a decoration, just as protective covering regularly used in the kitchen. Unlike the pony or the piano, these are not wrapped, because, like the poet's poem, they do not need to be.

What Caplow calls the "wrapping rule" was not manifest only in the paper and ribbon that people put on what they gave. It also shaped expectations about the display of presents and recording them in photographs: "The pile of wrapped gifts was photographed; and individual participants were photographed opening a gift, ideally at the moment of 'surprise'. Although the pile of wrapped gifts is almost invariably photographed, a heap of unwrapped gifts is not a suitable subject for the Christmas photographer" (Caplow 1984: 1311). That unwrapped heap would look too much like a pile of loot.

The last way of making commodities suitable to be Christmas presents is a form of appropriation that I have mentioned previously: the work of shopping. I said that this turns the impersonal items on display on the shelf in the shop or on the web page into things that I have selected, which makes them more personal, and I have selected them because I will consume them in social relationships of family, friends or flat-mates. In market-based societies, shopping is work that people do all year round. Because Christmas is a time when using commodities in personal relationships is central, it is appropriate that it is a time when people tell themselves how important that shopping is, how important it is to get the right gift.

It is also appropriate that it is a time when getting the right gift is said to be hard work. Complaints about the difficulty of drawing up the lists, battling the crowds, dealing with surly assistants in stores with their garish decorations or websites that keep crashing, trying to find the money – all of these stress that the appropriation is work. Although it is individuals who do that work, the newspaper stories and news reports and chat at the office or over coffee or a beer make it obvious that we are all in it together, that we are all engaged in the same task – a task that begins to look like a ritual. In a ritual, we take something that we do often and do it in a special way, so that it reflects and strengthens important common values and helps us to deal with an important common problem, even if only symbolically.

The common problem arises from the fact that Christmas is not just being at home with the family gathered around the tree, either in reality or in people's imagination. The affectionate world of home does not exist by itself but exists in its context. The tales about the work of shopping show that an important aspect of that context is the impersonal commercial world and the economic realm more generally, at least as they are rendered culturally as the world of what David Schneider calls work. From this perspective, then, Christmas is not just about home. Rather, it is about home as a haven in a heartless world.

This means that if we are to understand Christmas we need to recognize that it is not the day but is instead the ritual season, which includes the Christmas shopping. It is not just the family that is stressed and presented in intense terms at Christmas; so is the economic world in which it exists and to which it is opposed. As I have said, people negotiate the relationship between those two realms throughout the year. Once a year, however, they collectively celebrate and reaffirm their ability to do so. It is work, even hard work, but, when they struggle through the shopping and make it through Christmas day, they show themselves that they can do it.

The spirit of Christmas past

O. Henry invoked the three wise men, with their gifts of gold, frankincense and myrrh. This suggests that he thought that Christmas and giving are old, and in fact the Catholic Church had marked 25 December as the day of the birth of Christ by the onset of the Dark Ages. My approach implies a different history, one focused on social concerns, values and practices rather than ecclesiastical matters of the Church calendar.

I have portrayed Christmas as a ritual celebration and affirmation of affectionate familial and social life and values in the face of an outside world that differs from them and threatens them. The celebration is a response to the increasing separation of the realms of economy and society, which I said was first advocated in Anglophone countries by members of the Scottish Enlightenment late in the eighteenth century. My histories of changes in production and circulation described the spread and intensification of this separation, especially in the nineteenth century.

Effectively, this is the uneven rise of modern capitalism in different places and different areas of life in the United Kingdom and the United States. With that spread, the nature of gifts changes. Before the disembedding of economic activity from social life, people got the bulk of what they needed for survival through transactions in social relationships, in the manner of Ponam Islanders and people in English market towns. Jonathan Parry, an economic anthropologist, summarizes a pertinent consequence of that disembedding when he says that "as economic relations become increasingly differentiated from other types of social relationship [...] [g]ifts can ... be given the sole objective of cementing social relations" (1986: 466). With this the way is clear for the appearance of the pure gift, "altruistic, moral and loaded with emotion", and seen to be the opposite of transaction in the economic realm: self-interested, amoral and dispassionate.

England is the cultural precursor of the United States, and in England before the eighteenth century there were celebrations that look like Christmas, although they were around New Year rather than Christmas itself and differed from modern Christmas in significant ways. The celebrations involved giving and getting, and the scattered evidence indicates that two themes were fairly common: a stress on the quantity or value of what was given and a stress on hierarchy. Further, these presents did not circulate within the family but moved between people in different households. The gifts, then, were a long way from today's perfect present.

These combined in a regular feature of those celebrations, feasting, in which those attending should be presented with more food and drink than they possibly could consume. Commonly feasts were organized by superiors for their dependants, and in rural areas dependants would contribute to the feast, their contributions augmented by the landlord or notable who organized it. Their pattern, then, looks rather like what Polanyi called "redistribution". The two themes combined in a different way with year-end presents, and there were two sorts. One was among the gentry and nobility, and the flow of presents, and hence wealth, was upward, as nobles and officials received from their subordinates gifts of money or the equivalent in plate. Moreover, it appears as though the value of gifts was fairly standardized, depending on the status of giver and recipient. The other sort was gifts to subordinates, such as household staff or borough menials.

In the colonies that became the United States, year-end activities varied. In New England, Puritans were opposed to the festivities and tried to suppress them, with reasonable success. People in the American South, however, generally followed the English pattern of feasting and giving presents to menials, including gifts to slaves, usually of clothing. In contrast to England, however, year-end festivities were primarily an urban affair rather than a rural one.

England and the colonies differed as well in the ancillary features of those festivities, and by historical accident one of those features took on a new form that, ultimately, became recognizable as Santa Claus. This began in New York City, where, by the start of the 1770s, many people were celebrating the sixth of December rather than year's end. Those celebrations were not familial, however, but political. The sixth of December is St Nicholas Day, and the fact that the saint was supposed to be Dutch appealed to New Yorkers who were opposed to British rule of a city that was founded by the Dutch as New Amsterdam. It was political in another way as well, because it specifically was not Christmas, which was tarred by being a holy day on the Church of England calendar and an official British holiday.

St Nicholas, shortened to Santa Claus, remained important only in the city, but this changed. As one historian describes it, "Santa Claus was a local joke with an anti-British sting until 1809; after 1809 the spritely SC spread like the plague" (Jones 1978: 345). That was the year that Washington Irving published, pseudonymously, the book known as *Knickerbocker's History*, a somewhat fanciful account of the history of Dutch New Amsterdam that was very popular and had many references to the saint (Irving 1809).

The spread of the saint did not mean the spread of familial Christmas with presents to children. The most that they might get was seasonal sweets, associated with the saint in the Netherlands. In the 1820s celebration of Santa Claus moved to year's end and then to Christmas, helped in 1823 by the publication of Charles Clement Moore's popular poem "A visit from St Nicholas", commonly called "The night before Christmas". This poem not only stressed the 25th as the important day, it also encouraged the modern view of Santa Claus as bearded, fat and jolly, and hence different from his precursors, the Dutch St Nicholas and the English Father Christmas. In spite of these events, however, it remained the case that in the seat of American industry and commerce, New York City, festivities occurred indifferently at Christmas or New Year and the focus was adult feasting, with children rarely getting presents other than those sweets.

Another work is taken to be a classic, formative expression of modern Christmas: Charles Dickens's *A Christmas Carol*. It was published in 1843, and is still family Christmas reading for many. As Tom Lehrer puts it in that satirical song that I mentioned, "Mix the punch, drag out the Dickens / Even though the prospect sickens / Brother, here we go again." Given what I have said about the cultural opposition between the social and economic realms, it is understandable that modern interpretations of the book, typified by the movie *The Muppet Christmas Carol* (Muppets 1992), focus on Tiny Tim, Bob Cratchit and familial affection, and on their triumph over the calculating economic self-interest of Scrooge. This is a selective reading, however, of a work that in fact continues much of the focus on hierarchical relations outside the family and feasting of the older English year's end.

Hierarchy is important in a number of ways. It is apparent when Scrooge is revisiting Fezziwig's ball with the Ghost of Christmas Past and explains the importance of the ball to Fezziwig's employees: "He has the power to render us happy or unhappy; to make our service light or burdensome; a pleasure or a toil. Say that his power lies in words and looks; in things so slight and insignificant that it is impossible to add and count 'em up – what then? The happiness he gives is quite as great as if it cost a fortune" (Dickens 1918 [1843]: 78).

It is important in a different way when Scrooge's nephew tries to explain the meaning of Christmas, saying that it is the one time of the year "when men and women seem by one consent to open their shut-up hearts freely, and to think of people below them as if they really were fellow-passengers to the grave, and not another race of creatures bound on other journeys" (1918 [1843]: 14). In addition, it recurs in the book's invocation of the importance of impersonal charity toward one's inferiors. Many were advocating this sort of charity at the time, in part to counter the class tensions that were becoming important in the country with the spread of capitalist manufacturing and commerce. I have mentioned two depictions of these tensions. One is of the rural food riots late in the eighteenth century that E. P. Thompson (1971) describes. The other is of the conditions of those who worked for Henry Mayhew's show and slop-shops that sold cheap clothing in London in the 1840s, conditions against which they too rioted.

Feasting and a surfeit of food also are important in the book, as they were in popular English representations of Father Christmas at the time. Dickens described the room where the Ghost of Christmas Present appears:

> Heaped up on the floor, to form a kind of throne, were turkeys, geese, game, poultry, brawn, great joints of meat, suckling-pigs, long wreaths of sausages, mince-pies, plum-puddings, barrels of oysters, red-hot chestnuts, cherry-cheeked apples, juicy oranges, luscious pears, immense twelfth-cakes, and seething bowls of punch, that made the chamber dim with their delicious steam.
> (Dickens 1918 [1843]: 94)

And again, and at greater length, he (1918 [1843]: 99–100) described the opulent food that Scrooge sees when he is led around the streets by the Ghost to observe people spending Christmas.

The family and its sentiments that are the core of modern Christmas exist in *A Christmas Carol*, but the old themes of hierarchy and feasting remain strong. The most that one can say, then, is that the book marked the gradual emergence of the imagery and sentiment that the Muppets stressed and that are part of the season in the present. That emergence was uneven, and John Golby's description of English Christmas in the 1830s shows that the unevenness reflects different sets of people's exposure to and experience of the emerging impersonal economy, understood as different from the social realm. He says that only two groups had marked Christmas celebrations in that decade. The gentry celebrated it in the older style that I have described. The other group was those most exposed to the disembedded economy, the urban bourgeoisie, "the professional, clerical and shopkeeping classes" (Golby 1981: 16). Another historian, J. A. R. Pimlott (1978: chs 7, 8), says that it was they who provided the celebrants of familial Christmas and the enthusiastic readers of *A Christmas Carol*.

Once the ball started rolling, however, it moved quickly. In 1836 the first American state declared Christmas a public holiday, Puritan Massachusetts did so in 1855 and it became a national holiday in 1865. That period also saw the first images recognizable as the modern Santa Claus. They were by Thomas Nast and appeared, complete with presents and a Christmas tree, during the US Civil War in the periodical *Harper's Weekly*. The fully modern Santa Claus, however, had to wait for Coca-Cola advertisements in the 1930s (see Belk 1993: 77–89).

Knickerbocker's History, Charles Dickens, Thomas Nast and the rest are important for tracing the development of the symbolism of Christmas, but it is important not to be beguiled by the specifics of that symbolism. The symbols were real and had a force of their own, but they became popular because they resonated with what important groups of people were experiencing and thinking about, and it is likely that other symbols produced by different historical accidents would have done as well. This much is apparent in what Daniel Miller (1994: 83–107) says of Christmas in Trinidad. With its different history, many of the symbols of Christmas there are different. As he describes, however, the core focus on the family and familial ties, in contrast to what exists outside, is just as strong.

If we consider them using the concepts of economic anthropology, we can see that what those groups of people were experiencing was a world that seemed to be divided into the two realms of economy and society. Further, the historical changes in production and circulation sketched in previous chapters make it clear that what they experienced was becoming more common in the United States and the United Kingdom. Seen this way, Christmas in the full sense that I have assigned to it was a response to that experience – one that allowed people to celebrate the values of society, and especially the family, in the face of the threatening world of economy, and to affirm once again their ability to make home a haven in a heartless world.

7

Consumption and meaning

The countries that I know best have societies of mass consumption, and at its simplest this means that its members have a lot of stuff. They have so much that, as I noted previously, some people make a living telling them that they ought to have less, that they ought to declutter their lives and that they ought to give and value experiences rather than things. Seeing consumption as stuff accords with the economistic view of people in the market, which says that (a) people have desires, (b) if they have the money to do so they buy things that will satisfy those desires and (c) that is pretty much the end of the story.

Economic anthropologists interested in consumption view things differently, and for them the story does not end when people buy things. The buying is important, but they approach it in terms of the origin and nature of the desires and of the social and cultural context of what happens after our consumer brings the stuff home. Mary Douglas and Baron Isherwood (1978: 66–7) say that ignoring those desires and that context means that we would find it hard to distinguish the gourmet's meal from "solitary feeding, where the person wolfs or bolts his food, probably standing by his refrigerator in his overcoat".

"What happens after our consumer brings the stuff home" covers a vast range of activity. Indeed, some have complained that the term covers so much that it is effectively meaningless; for a long time my working definition of "consumption" was "not production". This means that what I say of work on consumption by economic anthropologists has to be very selective. One could invoke Douglas and Isherwood's (1978: 57) definition: "[A] use of material possessions that is beyond commerce and free within the law." That has the authority of Douglas's stature in anthropology, but it is remarkably vague and its use of "material" and "possessions" is more restrictive than many would like. After all, a person at a concert can reasonably be said to be consuming music, even though the music is neither material nor the listener's possession. The definition does indicate, however, that for economic anthropologists the term carries no particular connotation of using things up.

Ordering consumption

Douglas wrote on many topics, but running through them is a concern with how people's activities express an order and impose it on the world, even if only imperfectly. Further, the person who does those things is not the isolated, autonomous individual of neoclassical economics, satisfying the desire for food by solitary feeding. Rather, that person exists in relationships with others. That person's activities are influenced by the activities and talk of those others. Likewise, the order does not exist simply in the individual's mind. Rather, it is public, visible to and an influence on all, for it is made visible and concrete by public activities and the talk that accompanies them.

In perhaps her most famous book, *Purity and Danger* (1966), Douglas pursues this interest in conceptual order and its expression in people's lives. The book is a consideration of how we can study religions comparatively, which may seem a long way from consumption. Douglas says that all religions enjoin people to do some things and not to do others, however, and those injunctions identify what is proper and improper, clean and unclean, pure and impure, and hence include what people should and should not consume. For her, these injunctions are ways of imposing order on the world. As she (1966: 4) puts it, "Ideas about separating, purifying, demarcating and punishing transgressions have as their main function to impose system on an inherently untidy experience."

In the Bible, this is the focus of Leviticus 11 in the Old Testament, which reports the words of the Lord spoken to Moses and Aaron, concerning what they can and cannot eat. Referring to beasts that dwell on the land, verses 1 to 8 in the New King James Version have:

> 1 Now the Lord spoke to Moses and Aaron, saying to them, 2 Speak to the children of Israel, saying, "These are the animals which you may eat among all the animals that are on the earth: 3 Among the

animals, whatever divides the hoof, having cloven hooves and chewing the cud – that you may eat. 4 Nevertheless these you shall not eat among those that chew the cud or those that have cloven hooves: the camel, because it chews the cud but does not have cloven hooves, is unclean to you; 5 the rock hyrax, because it chews the cud but does not have cloven hooves, is unclean to you; 6 the hare, because it chews the cud but does not have cloven hooves, is unclean to you; 7 and the swine, though it divides the hoof, having cloven hooves, yet does not chew the cud, is unclean to you. 8 Their flesh you shall not eat, and their carcasses you shall not touch. They are unclean to you.

Referring to things that live in the water, verses 9 to 12 have:

9 These you may eat of all that are in the water: whatever in the water has fins and scales, whether in the seas or in the rivers – that you may eat. 10 But all in the seas or in the rivers that do not have fins and scales, all that move in the water or any living thing which is in the water, they are an abomination to you. 11 They shall be an abomination to you; you shall not eat their flesh, but you shall regard their carcasses as an abomination. 12 Whatever in the water does not have fins or scales – that shall be an abomination to you.

These injunctions have long attracted scholarly interest: lumping together the camel, the hare and the pig seems to make no sense. Douglas describes various efforts to make sense of them, especially the materialist. In that, scholars look for what strike us as the beneficial material consequences that the injunctions have. For instance, defining pigs as unclean is taken to reflect the dangers of eating pork in hot climates. To say that heeding the injunction has the effect of reducing people's exposure to that danger does not, however, explain why the injunction was laid down in the first place; neither does it account for enjoining the camel and the hare. Douglas (1966: 29) rejects this sort of approach: "Even if some of Moses's dietary rules were hygienically beneficial it is a pity to treat him as an enlightened public health administrator, rather than as a spiritual leader."

She thinks it better to treat the injunctions as a rejection of dirt. As she (1966: 35) explains it, dirt entails two things: a system of order and a violation of that order. Further, the violation can be contextual rather than absolute. For most of us, shoes in and of themselves are not dirty. They would be dirty, however, if they were in the wrong context – for instance, if we put them on the dinner table.

Douglas (1966: ch. 3) uses this approach in an extended consideration of those injunctions and of scholarly attempts to explain them. In doing so, she relates them to other parts of Leviticus and of the Pentateuch, the first five books of the Bible, which is also the Torah. She uses the injunctions as indications of what things are considered dirty, which in turn are clues about the order that those dirty things violate. She argues that the biblical texts link observing the injunctions to holiness, which has two aspects in the Pentateuch. One concerns the nature of particular things and types. Things that are clean are complete and whole and are full representatives of their type. As she (1966: 54) puts it, "To be holy is to be whole, to be one; holiness is unity, integrity, perfection of the individual and of the kind." The other aspect of holiness is that signs of it and the observances associated with it, like the injunctions in Leviticus, regularly remind believers of God, who laid them down, and of the completeness and wholeness that is holiness.

In this chapter of *Purity and Danger*, Douglas describes how Leviticus assigns meanings to things, as clean and unclean, as fit to consume (or even touch) or not. She does so in order to show how those meanings rest on a conception of the world as ordered, made up of individual beings that are more or less whole and complete and that more or less adequately represent types of beings. Those that are not whole, such as a calf born with only three legs, are unclean. The same is true of those that do not adequately represent their type, such as animals that have cloven hooves but do not chew the cud, for "[c]loven-hoofed, cud-chewing ungulates are the model of the proper kind of food for a pastoralist" (Douglas 1966: 54). For her, then, Leviticus is a system of meaning and is important for showing how people create and impose a cosmological order on what is, as she says, an inherently untidy experience.

Other anthropologists have been concerned with how consumption is related to different and less profound meanings and orderings. They are the sorts of meanings that set this brand of soup or this holiday resort off from that one. Edward Fischer (e.g. 2020) has studied this in terms of what is called third-wave coffee. The first wave is the ordinary coffee of my youth, sold in tins on supermarket shelves and made in the percolator at home. The second wave marked a shift from coffee as a familiar hot drink to something to be thought about and valued, most visible in the spread of chains such as Starbucks. In the third wave that thinking and value are strengthened with a concern for what variety of coffee was grown at what altitude by which farmer in what country, how it was roasted and turned into what is in the cup. This is encapsulated in an idea of quality, elaborated and formalized with the development of protocols and standards for defining and assessing it by organizations such as the Specialty Coffee Association and the search for coffee with a cupping score of 90 or even 95. These coffees are scarce and expensive, with prices often 20 or more times that of standard coffee on the New York coffee markets.

Why do people pay that much for a cup of coffee? I said that these coffees are presented in terms of quality, but quality is a murky concept to apply to what is in the cup. One way that anthropologists have sought to answer this sort of question is in terms of the public meanings and relationships of consumption. These are different from the cosmological ordering that Douglas describes, as well as from the private meanings and relationships that are important in understanding gifts and possessions, which are linked to particular people in particular relationships with each other that have particular histories.

Communication about the self

Probably the best-known invocation of those public meanings and relationships is in the idea of conspicuous consumption, described by an American economist, Thorstein Veblen, around 1900.

Veblen argued that a central aspect of consumption, and of ownership more generally, is social: people's desire to show that they differ from others by the display of wealth, the "unremitting demonstration of the ability to pay" (Veblen 1927 [1899]: 87). He argued, moreover, that the need for such demonstration is itself social. That is because, in smaller and more stable groups, people are known to each other so that they know who has wealth and who does not. As groups become larger and more complex, however, that sort of personal knowledge disappears. Consequently, members are increasingly likely to confront strangers whom they can judge only by appearances, the things that they display and the wealth that it signifies – such as a very expensive cup of coffee in a coffee shop of the right sort.

As Veblen described it, conspicuous consumption is unidimensional. People are ranked on a single variable, their wealth, and what people consume is related to that same variable. However important this may be, it is obvious that consumption is more complex than that. This is apparent in sumptuary laws, which defined who could have what. Such laws existed in Europe from the time of ancient Greece and served different purposes in different times and places. In Western Europe in the later medieval and early modern period, however, they sought to place limits on the effects of Veblen's ability to pay, which meant that the laws reflected the view that things other than wealth are also important in shaping what it is that people can consume.

In England, for instance, economic change meant that some people of no particular social standing acquired enough wealth to emulate their superiors, and, indeed, the borders between social groups in the country often were unstable. From what Neil McKendrick and his colleagues (McKendrick *et al.* 1982: ch. 2) describe, there were regular complaints that servants aped their masters, that their masters aped the gentry and that the gentry aped the nobility. Sumptuary laws tried to prevent this, and so had two aspects. One was the definition of a hierarchy of social groups and the other was the restriction of the consumption of certain things to certain of those groups.

This association of consumption and social standing is no longer embodied in law, although it was in the United States until the end of legal racial segregation. It continues to exist in practice, however, although it is not commonly presented in terms of social status or the ability to pay. Rather, in an echo of the economistic view of market transactors, it tends to be understood in terms of personal likes and dislikes: taste. And, as we all know, *de gustibus non est disputandum*. Viewing it this way raises a question. If tastes are personal, how does it come about that different likes and dislikes are visibly associated with different degrees of status and wealth?

One answer is in *Distinction*, Pierre Bourdieu's study of taste in France in the 1960s (Bourdieu 1984 [1979]). He argues that the more one goes up the social scale the more likely people are to evaluate things in terms of criteria other than their immediate human content as they exist in people's lives. This is one aspect of what he sees as a broader relationship between social class and a concern with aesthetics, which is a tendency to step back from immediate sensual perception in concrete circumstances and, instead, approach things in terms of more abstract and impersonal frames.

For instance, describing people's responses to photographs, Bourdieu (1984 [1979]: 45) says that people in the lower social realms tend to evaluate them in terms of how what is portrayed in the photograph would look in their everyday lives: "I wouldn't like that photograph in my house, in my room. It isn't very nice to look at." Those higher up the scale are likely to take a more distanced view in which the photograph is perceived in terms other than its immediate and personal material context: "It could be a Dreyer character, Bergman at a pinch, or perhaps even Eisenstein, in *Ivan the Terrible* ... I like it a lot" (1984 [1979]: 45–6, ellipsis in original).

The contrasting approaches to photographs illustrate contrasting approaches to what one can call the personal: one's self and one's ordinary surroundings. The lower-status person points to the personal explicitly, referring to "my house" and "my room". The higher-status person locates the photograph in relation to something more public and divorced from the everyday: films by Dreyer, Bergman, maybe even Eisenstein. This distance from the everyday and personal appears as well with those third-wave coffees. They are construed in terms of their quality, and the protocols of tasting and scoring that Fischer describes presuppose that quality is public and objective, outside the individual's immediate life and perceptions. This means that to say that a coffee has a very high cupping score, that it has subtle and complex aroma and an aftertaste of a particular sort, is to locate it in an abstract frame. Such a coffee is likely be interesting and even intriguing to those who know and care about such things. The high score by itself says nothing, however, about how much one would like a cup of it at breakfast.

Bourdieu's identifying people in terms of class indicates that he does not see the tendency to the aesthetic as simply a matter of personal predilection, randomly distributed among a set of people. Rather, he argues that it varies with people's social location. As he puts it:

> The true basis of the differences found in the area of consumption, and far beyond it, is the opposition between the tastes of luxury (or freedom) and the tastes of necessity. The former are the tastes of individuals who are the product of material conditions of existence defined by distance from necessity ... the latter express ... the necessities of which they are the product.   (1984 [1979]: 177)

In linking taste and consumption to social class in this way, Bourdieu is unpacking what economists generally treat as taken for granted and exogenous to their models, what they call people's preferences or utility functions, which are what the rest of us call their likes and dislikes. Bourdieu's unpacking does not make those preferences less real for the people involved, and he argues that their reality comes from socialization, the lives of which they are, he says, the product. People are brought up in families and broader social settings in which things are seen to have particular meanings and associations, so that certain sorts of things are valued positively and others negatively. As a result, people internalize those values and make them their own, just as I still value the sorts of furniture, pictures and clothing that surrounded me when I was growing up. Obviously tastes change over the course of people's lives, but those changes are not random. Rather, they are shaped by people's past in two senses. One is the tastes that people had in the past, which are the context and foundation of those changes. The other is the social settings in which they find themselves as their tastes change, settings shaped by their upbringing and past.

As I have described, Bourdieu is concerned with the social factors that shape people's taste, their perception of objects and hence their propensity to consume them. For him, then, those factors and the structure of society that encompasses them are reflected to some degree in the distribution of taste. One consequence of this is that the distribution of taste becomes self-evident and so is reproduced. If, because of their background and social setting, upper-middle-class people in, say, urban areas in the American South like certain sorts of food, then there will be an empirical association between them and their diets. This will be apparent to neutral observers as an objective fact: anyone can see that those people tend to eat that kind of food. With this, social factors of the sort that Bourdieu describes slip from view. Instead, the association of these people and their food becomes part of the natural order of things, and that tends to reproduce the association of people and taste as a simple fact of life.

The result of this is something like what Bourdieu (1977 [1972]: 164) calls misrecognition, in which a society engages in "the naturalization of its own arbitrariness". The arbitrariness involved is social practices and beliefs, and the social patterns that they produce, which are human creations rather than naturally given, just as the score that defines the quality of this or that cup of coffee is a human creation. That, after all, is a function of the particular assessment techniques that people such as those in the Specialty Coffee Association devise. The naturalization is seeing these as natural or just as objective facts of life, which ignores the way that they are arbitrary, are human creations that could be otherwise.

When those practices and beliefs work to the advantage of some people rather than others, they are engines of inequality, and naturalizing them treats the inequality as natural. In my youth in the United States, for instance, some argued that integrating schools was wrong-headed because Black children are not as intelligent as White children, and so need separate schooling. They justified this by pointing to the lower average educational attainment of Black children compared to White children, which they naturalized by treating it as a matter of natural endowment rather than the way that schools and teaching practices were organized and funded, not to mention other practices and beliefs that affected Black people and White people differently and that could have been otherwise.

If such arguments become entrenched they produce "the *sense of limits*, commonly called the *sense of reality*" (Bourdieu 1977 [1972]: 164, emphasis in original), whereby people's desires and expectations end up corresponding to their objective chances in the existing social system. So, in the time of my youth it would have been unrealistic for Black people to aspire to become, say, Wall Street investment bankers, just as, later, beliefs about women's mentality would have made it unrealistic for girls to want to grow up to become physicists or engineers. Their sense of reality meant that they would not even try, and the pertinent aspects of the social order and their place in it would be reproduced.

Communication about others

Bourdieu focuses on the social mechanisms that shape taste, and so directs our attention to what people like and consume. To a degree this echoes the economistic focus on preferences, even though he does not at all take those preferences for granted. Jean Baudrillard (1981 [1968]) carries this one step further. Drawing on Claude Lévi-Strauss's (1969 [1962]) analysis of totemism, he presents a model that puts people, likes and objects in a more complex social and cultural frame.

A totem is a semi-sacred object to which a group of people stand in a special relationship, and a society with totemism has a number of such groups, each with its own totem. Researchers have long attempted to make sense of this, mostly focusing on the relationship between the group and its totem. Why, for example, do the people of the bear clan have the bear as their totem? These attempts often look at what things are, specifically the real or symbolic attributes of the totem and how they were related to the attributes of the clan. In this, those attempts resemble Bourdieu's analysis of taste: what are the attributes of, for example, modern art and those who like it? For him, as I have said, that art appeals to those people because it fits with the distanced aesthetic of those who like it, just as the subtle aroma and flavours detected in third-wave coffee fit with the aesthetic of those who drink it.

Lévi-Strauss argues that, when they worried about that relationship between bears and the bear clan, researchers were asking the wrong question. In totemic societies, to continue this hypothetical example, the bear clan and their bears do not exist by themselves but coexist with, say, the eagle clan and their eagles. For Lévi-Strauss, we need to take that coexistence into account. We need to ask how people's understandings of the differences between bears and eagles relate to their understandings of the differences between the bear clan and the eagle clan.

So, instead of looking at what the bear and the bear clan are and at the relationship defined by their similarities, we need to look at what they are not and at the relationship defined by their differences from other totems and other clans. We may find out that people say something like this: "We of the bear clan are not like eagles, which are creatures of the air, fierce hunters and quick to anger, as are members of the eagle clan. Rather, we, like bears, are creatures of the earth, strong, patient and industrious, which eagles and members of that clan are not." Moreover, for Lévi-Strauss those differences are themselves encompassed by a set of broader oppositions: air versus earth, quick versus slow to anger, hunting and seizing things versus industriously making them.

When he applies Lévi-Strauss to consumption, Baudrillard is telling us that what people do not consume can be important. Some non-consumption is dull and uninteresting: I do not eat iguana eggs, but that is only because I have never been in a place where they were available and so have never had the chance to see them as possible food. Some, however, is interesting. Richard Wilk (1994), an anthropologist interested in consumption and long an avid fisher, points to this. He says that when he grew up in New England, the northeasternmost part of the United States, people loathed catfish and said that they are inedible (to recall Leviticus, many catfish have no scales). When, later, he was fishing in Florida, he was understandably surprised to learn that catfish are considered nice to eat. In Florida he also learned that tarpon and bonefish were good sport fishing, but were not really edible. Later still, in Belize, people told him that they are tasty food, while catfish are disgusting. It is apparent from what he says that all three fish are edible at the biological level and that the people he fished with were familiar with them but that they had markedly different assessments of them as food.

Wilk suggests that non-consumption has not attracted much scholarly attention because disciplinary views of consumption tend to reflect the common economic focus on wanting and getting. This makes not wanting and forgoing almost invisible, although there is increasing work on related things such as degrowth. The low level of scholarly interest is unfortunate, for it encourages us to attend to those third-wave coffees and those who consume them, while ignoring those who are happy with second- or even first-wave sorts and do not want to change.

Baudrillard's invocation of Lévi-Strauss helps correct this, and Wilk's description of attitudes toward catfish in New England helps explain how it does so. Wilk says that he was told that only Black people and poor people ate them. In other words, the structure of taste, which is the structure of people's understanding of objects, can resemble the structure of society. Just as the relationship between bears and eagles resembles the relationship between the bear clan and the eagle clan, so the relationship between large-mouth bass and catfish resembles the relationship between proper, desirable people – the ones Wilk talked to – and the improper, undesirable ones: the poor and the Black.

The relationship between consumption and social status need not be so hierarchical as it seems to be in the minds of those New England fishers, but it is the case that commonly we are presented with the moralized equation of different sorts of consumption and different sorts of people. A recent, striking instance of this in Britain is people who were called chavs, in Scotland often neds (a comparable group in the United States would be those called trailer trash). Chavs were seen to be working-class and poorly educated White youth (Jones 2011). They were represented as having distinctive tastes in clothing, especially adornment called bling and the hoodie, the term for a sweatshirt with an attached hood but often used to refer to the sort of people who are taken to wear them. Chavs also were seen to drink too much, and because they were fairly poor it was cheap alcohol, often cider but also some stronger beers. These often were called "wife beaters", because of their assumed association with domestic violence, in turn assumed to be associated with chavs. In Baudrillard's terms, the structure of taste and consumption mapped on to the structure of society and evaluated the elements of those structures morally.

This sort of moral structuring of taste and society has long been around, illustrated by William Hogarth's *Gin Lane*, a print published in 1751. It portrays the evils of cheap alcohol in the form of gin, and does so in terms of public drunkenness in a slum area of London. The consumption and behaviour of the poor people that he portrays would have repelled those likely to buy the print – people likely to frequent the more respectable coffee houses popular at the time. This sort of structuring is especially visible when the boundaries around social groups and membership in them are changing.

In the United States, marijuana was long associated with Black people and those who consorted with them. In the 1930s the prolonged trials of the Scottsboro Boys, which led to rising discontent with all-White Southern juries, and the passage by the House in 1937 of the Gavagan anti-lynching bill (which died in the Senate) indicated that the older forms of racial control were weakening. Appropriately, it was late in that decade that marijuana was banned by the federal government, when the Marihuana Tax Act became law, after hearings that included "overtly racist rhetoric" (Polson 2018: 144). Such moralization of consumption is not automatic, however. In the face of the rapid spread of opioid misuse in the United States, users commonly are said to be weak and despairing, different from the amoral, corrupting hedonists of earlier portrayals of marijuana users. But, then, those who misuse opioids generally are seen to be White.

Moral structuring of taste and consumption also can occur when new social groups are emerging, and Melanie Archer and Judith Blau (1993) address this in their survey of work on the emergence and changing nature of the urban middle class in the United States in the nineteenth century. They describe the spread of a set of refined tastes and attitudes "that was both the expression and legitimization of middle-class behavior and ideals" (1993: 30). Because this class was not yet really established, people who thought that they ought to be seen as members were uncertain about how they ought to be acting and thinking, which was important if others were to recognize them as members. It is understandable, then, that in the period after the US Civil War a wave of periodicals and books told people what middle-class refinement was and how to enact and possess it. And refinement was, of course, not neutral but contained a moral evaluation. Those who did not have it were contemptible and even dangerous. The growing and changing middle class and their concern for refinement was accompanied by spreading nativism, which cast immigrants as drunken, Catholic louts who threatened sober, Protestant American society.

Those uncertain members of the American middle class with their concern for refinement were not simply trying to locate themselves in a desirable place in society and protect that society and themselves from threat. In doing those things they also were defining themselves in opposition to those immigrants, just as members of the British middle class were defining themselves in opposition to chavs. This takes Baudrillard's argument that the relationships between objects and between people reflect each other and extends it into the realm of class politics and the debate about which people consume in ways that mark them as among the proper members of society and which people ought to be excluded because their consumption puts them beyond the pale.

This sort of definition by opposition, or dialectical definition, occurs when two things are defined not in terms of their own attributes but in terms of their differences from each other, such as the difference between the bear clan and the eagle clan or between those who do and do not eat catfish. So, in Italy, many in the north of the country contrast themselves with those from the south. Northerners are industrious, plan ahead, are educated and intelligent, are law-abiding; southerners are lazy, have no thought for the future, are ignorant and stupid, are criminal. In this, those northerners identify themselves not simply in terms of what they are, or what they think that they are, but in terms of what they are not. And what they are not is what southerners are, or what those northerners think that they are. Similarly, public concern about chavs associated a set of consumption preferences that amount to a style of life with a sort of person, but it also encouraged those who were concerned about chavs to evaluate themselves positively, for they wore proper clothing, drank responsibly, ate a proper diet rather than junk food, and so on: they had a good style of life.

This definition by opposition has consequences, and attending to them helps us to understand patterns of and talk about consumption in society. One echoes what Lévi-Strauss and Baudrillard say. A set of people may be defined in terms of what they do, but what they do becomes a focus of attention because it differs from other sets of people who do other things. This means that activities that are not seen to distinguish groups tend to be uninteresting and drop from view. So, chavs and respectable British people both drink water, get sick from time to time and shop for groceries, but no one mentions this. A second consequence is a kind of simplification, a tendency to assume that all members of each group do, or are prone to do, the same things. All chavs drink too much, or would if they had the money, just as all respectable Britons drink moderately, if at all. And these two consequences combine to produce a third. No one in one group does what the opposed group is seen to do: no chav drinks a nice Petrus 2016, much less abstains from alcohol; no member of the respectable middle class eats junk food and drinks cheap cider. This illustrates the ramifications of Kenneth Burke's (1969: 34) reminding us of "a grim little pleasantry that runs, 'Of course we're Christians – but what are we being Christians *against?*' "

Mary Douglas was concerned with Leviticus, and we seem to have moved a long way from that. She was also concerned, however, with how judgements about consumption reflect and generate an important order; how things that violate that order are unclean, are dirt; and how those who consume those things themselves are unclean. Talk about chavs and what they consume is linked in no obvious way to the order of creation. It is, however, something that reflects and generates what many people see as another order: that of society in its proper form. We have not, then, moved very far from Leviticus after all.

8

Consumption in context

I have shown how consumption reflects and makes meaning. Whether we intend it or not, whether we are conscious of it or not, what we know or are told of who consumes what serves to divide the people and things around us into different groups, which often carry evaluations and even moral loads. These groupings, meanings and associated evaluations are public, in the sense that they are what we see in movies and on television and what we read in the newspapers and on the web. They are, in a way, what everybody knows.

Of course, there is more to consumption than the expression and reproduction of public meanings. When we consume things, personal meanings and relationships also are important. They arise from our dealings with and use of different things in different contexts with different people. Economic anthropologists are some of those who have described these things and how they can be important for understanding consumption.

Consuming for social relations

Consumption routinely occurs in social relations, and it should be no surprise that it can affect and reflect those relations. This is the point that Mary Douglas and Baron Isherwood pursue in *The World of Goods*. There they do battle with economists about why people consume the things that they do. Is it price? If so, why does the demand for some goods go down when the price goes up, while for others the demand does not change much and for yet a few others the demand goes up? Alternatively, is it the utility of things: how their properties mesh with people's wants and needs? Perhaps – but which wants and needs? Douglas and Isherwood have an answer. For them (1978: 111), "there is only one type of physical property of consumption goods that need be considered: the capacity of goods to increase personal availability".

By that they mean that goods are valued to the degree that they allow people to interact with others. Those others can be members of the household, friends or casual acquaintances. They even can be strangers, to whom one wants to appear a proper or even desirable fellow being, a suitable candidate for interaction. The importance of this interaction intrudes on us regularly. It appears in advertisements, when products are portrayed among a group of people who are friends enjoying themselves with the advertised ware in each other's company. It appears on the display of large candy bars at a supermarket near me, which tells us that the bars are good for sharing. Those advertisements and displays are sending a lot of different messages, but one of them is sheer interaction with others.

Some objects facilitate interaction with others directly. For instance, Facebook can do so, but only if a lot of people whom you know use it. Douglas and Isherwood (1978: 99–100) point to an instance of this, concerning telephones in England in the 1950s. In 1958 only a sixth of English households had a telephone, which had been around a long time, while just over a half owned a television, a fairly recent consumer product. As late as 1973 fewer than a half of households had a telephone. Televisions were fairly evenly spread across the different classes in 1958, but not telephones. Over two-thirds of those in the professional and managerial classes had one, compared to a quarter of ordinary white-collar workers and only a twentieth of blue-collar workers. For those blue-collar workers, social life tended to revolve around the workplace, the shops and the pub, which meant that people had little use for a telephone, and when they did need one they could go to a call box and use a public telephone. Because they had little use for one, they did not have one. And because the people whom they knew did not have one either, telephones did not facilitate interaction, so there was no point in them.

Although telephones and things such as Facebook facilitate social interaction directly, other objects can facilitate it indirectly, by allowing people the time that they need to organize and engage in it. With a refrigerator and freezer, people need to go shopping less frequently than they would otherwise. More to the point, because they can store perishable items, those who have one do not need to go to the shops during the day when they plan on entertaining people in the evening. Equally, dishwashers probably save time for all those who own them. That time can be especially important for a household that entertains a lot, however, whereas it may well be unimportant for one that entertains little.

Consuming in social relations

Things that people consume are not valued only in terms of how they facilitate social interaction. They are valued as well in terms of how they reflect social relations. As I have described in a previous chapter, the things that people transact with each other reflect and can affect the relationship between them. Equally, the things that members of a group have in common or share reflect and can affect relations among members and their self-conception. The group that I focus on here is the household, which has attracted substantial scholarly attention.

At the most general level, the things that the household acquires and the ways that they are arranged and displayed reflect, and so express, the way that the household sees itself. This expression is to some degree directed outward, showing to others what the household is, or claims to be. This can be Veblen's conspicuous consumption: the swimming pool in the back and the large windows revealing expensive furniture express wealth, as do the two or three fancy cars parked in the drive. Many other things can also be expressed, however, such as religious belief, athleticism, political orientation, and so on.

This expression is also inevitably directed inward, saying to household members "This is who we are" as a collectivity. The people in the household are part of that collectivity, but also they are individuals. So, such statements may be fragile, reflecting contentions in the relationship between them.

That contention is likely to reflect gender and age differences, and it can do so in fairly conscious or overt ways. This would be the case if, for instance, the kitchen, including what goes on there and what is produced there and served to household members, is seen as female and the realm of the wife and mother in the household. Henrike Donner provides an example of this among middle-class, high-caste households in Kolkata, formerly Calcutta. As she (2015: 145) describes it, preparing meals for the family "from scratch on a regular basis is the task of middle-class housewives", married women with children. For these families, food is important for expressing social identity in a variety of ways, and the meals are hard work. These women are in fairly well-to-do families, however, so they do not labour alone; rather, they are likely to work alongside their mothers-in-law and one or more servants. Nonetheless, "it is the mother who is praised again and again for preparing a meal 'with her own hands'", a meal that embodies her status and authority in the household as one who is important for maintaining a valued way of life.

Such a meal proclaims to the family and to others the status of the household and the central position of the mother in it, but the different members of the household can view that act of consumption and the authority of the mother differently. As Donner describes it, many younger people, especially boys, had different consumption preferences. They liked the food found in stylish shopping malls and in restaurants and takeaways, tokens of an attractive cosmopolitan modernity, and they were less wedded to the more traditional meals of the household. Such foods were a long way from what their mothers were praised for cooking, which raised the possibility of conflict between mothers and fathers, sons and daughters. Usually, Donner says, parents yielded to their children's demands at least some of the time.

Doing so, however, meant that mothers had to break some important consumption rules. Proper meals are prepared from scratch, whereas the new tastes require ingredients that are already processed, such as pasta, and such ingredients conventionally were said to mark those who were too lazy to cook properly. Moreover, some of the new tastes could be satisfied only if the household ate meat. This was particularly desired by sons, and it violated the long association of being high caste and being vegetarian. In this household dispute about consumption, then, the meals that the family ate may have proclaimed "who we are", but that proclamation reflected conflicts along age and gender lines, and revealed a weakening of the authority of the mother as an important keeper of high-caste, middle-class status.

The question of "who we are" appears as well in the consumption of electronic media and smartphones. There is public concern about their use, especially their use by the young, with different studies showing that use does (or does not) have a noticeable negative effect on their intellectual performance and emotional state. Being caring parents concerned with the well-being of their children, a number of important people have, it seems, restricted their children's use of such devices, including Steve Jobs when he was head of Apple, Evan Williams, a founder of Twitter, and a number of other men in the IT sector (Bilton 2014). Such restrictions may be cast in terms that appear more objective and scientific than what underlies the virtue of the home-cooked meals that Donner's mothers prepared, but the two are alike in using consumption to state to the family and the outside world "This is who we are". And, in both cases, that statement is shaped by the differences in the authority of different family members, just as it reflects gender: food is a feminine realm in the Kolkata middle classes and IT is a masculine realm in the United States.

Gender identities and relations can be important for influencing consumption in a way that is more implicit than disagreements about what a Kolkata mother ought to cook for dinner or what an IT father ought to allow his children to use and watch. This occurs when there are empirical differences between the ways that men and women think about and experience objects in their lives, even though those ways are not explicitly thought of as masculine or feminine by household members, or even recognized. This is illustrated by a study that Mihaly Csikszentmihalyi and Eugene Rochberg-Halton carried out among families in Chicago and the ways that household members thought about different objects in their lives, and here I restrict myself to what they say of adults, for adolescents and those of retirement age normally thought about things in other ways.

The authors find that those adult men and women tended to approach things differently, a difference that does not appear to have been articulated by the people they studied. Men commonly approached objects in terms of how the properties of a thing relate to the purposes and goals of the person who uses it. For example, they interviewed a policeman, who talked about what he called his "working tools", his guns. He said that

> guns to a policeman are like a horse to a jockey, you got to get used to them, work them a lot, know what they are capable of, know their strength and weaknesses, how it does what it does, every gun is different. A gun is not just something that makes a loud noise. The policeman who knows his job, he knows his gun too, so with a new gun it takes a lot of breaking in.
> (Csikszentmihalyi & Rochberg-Halton 1981: 108)

Women were less likely to approach things this way. Rather, much more than men they saw things in terms of the social relationships that they embodied. For example, one woman talked about what a quilt meant to her, which her relatives had made and given: "It means my whole family, that we all enjoy receiving these things … And if somebody makes it and puts so much time in it, to me it's love that's been put into the object … that's more special to me than anything … if you know how many hours are put into it" (1981: 143, ellipses in original). These gender differences may be easy to accommodate, perhaps with the man having a work room and the woman a separate room of her own. Even if they are accommodated, however, they will shape the ways that men and women see their household and the things within it, as well as the new things that one or the other of them might want to have in it.

In his detailed study of a household in north London, occupied by a family he calls the Simons, Eric Hirsch (1992) shows more explicitly how gender and social relations can affect consumption. The Simons were an adult couple, the man a computer specialist and the woman a school-teacher. They had five children, two of them adopted, and the two adults had definite views about what they wanted their family to be. They valued a fairly egalitarian, communal cohesiveness and a creative life rather than one of passive consumption. As Hirsch finds, things that did not fit with their values were allowed to fall into disrepair and ultimately were abandoned.

This is most clear with a computer that the parents had bought from a friend so that their children could play computer games. They initially had thought that this would be a good thing to have in the household. As it turned out, however, the sons came to use the computer in an individual-istic and competitive way, challenging each other for best score and crowing when they won, and complaining when they thought that they were not getting enough time to play with it. In addition, when they were playing on the computer the sons systematically excluded their two sisters. Based on this, the parents decided to abandon the computer. When it broke they did not get it fixed but, instead, finally bought a different computer with what they wanted: not games but creative software that the children could use for drawing and graphic design.

I have described some of the ways that anthropologists have approached consumption in the household. Those ways show that consumption is not a matter of individual desire but is shaped by, and shapes, the social relations that link household members, as well as their sense of who they are and who they ought to be. Those ways also show how age and gender can shape people's relations with regard to consumption and even their tastes.

Consuming for gain

I have described some of what economic anthropologists have said about consumption in the household and the ways that it is part of creating, maintaining and challenging the household as a coherent unit. People also consume other than in the household with those who are not members.

Such consumption can be a source of tension, for it takes members away from the household and so can be a threat to its social unity. Moreover, those involved in that consumption spend time and money that members might think ought to be devoted to the household. This can become a matter of public concern, especially among the middle classes, who have long stressed their domestic orientation as something that distinguishes them from the lower and upper classes. This concern is apparent in temperance movements. Campaigners regularly complained that men out drinking are ignoring their family obligations and wasting their pay, with songs such as "Come home, father" (Work 1864), which begins: "Father, dear father, come home with me now / The clock on the steeple strikes one."

Aside from the working-class bars and saloons that temperance campaigners attacked, more respectable people have consumed in social settings outside the household for centuries. There were the coffee houses in England that flourished in the seventeenth and eighteenth centuries, and the tea rooms that were popular starting in the nineteenth century. In these, people ate and drank in a social setting away from home and household members. Anthropologists call this sort of social consumption commensality and see it as a way that people can create and maintain social relations. These relations can be important for people's economic activities, and the way that they are so illustrates again the limitations of the economistic view of economy in terms of markets full of autonomous actors. A story from Jamaica can help explain this.

I was doing research on people involved in the country's coastal waters around 2004. At one point I was in a taxi in Port Antonio, on the northeast coast. The driver asked me how he could generate more business. He said that he had advertised in local publications and put things on the web, with no real effect. Thinking about it afterwards, I decided that his potential customers were likely to be fairly well off, as ordinary people would have walked or taken what was called a route taxi: cars operating as buses on regular routes. The fairly well off who were local and used taxis would have regular drivers. That left visitors, such as me, who would ask the hotel where they were staying or the restaurant where they were eating to telephone for a taxi. The problem that this driver faced was that there were a lot of drivers like him, and they all had left their cards at the hotels and restaurants in town. Why should the person telephoning for a taxi pick his card out of the dozen or so in the pile on the desk? The most obvious reason is that the person knew the driver and liked him well enough to put business his way.

For that taxi driver in Port Antonio, as for many others closer to home, not everything looks like the impersonal market that we tell ourselves that we confront. Some of the economic realms that we experience are that impersonal, as anyone going into a large supermarket or buying something on the web can attest. It is pertinent that these are situations in which we want to buy something. On the other hand, when it comes to selling, all that most of us have to offer is our labour or perhaps our services. Then, we are like that taxi driver, and things can look different.

Economists tell us that there is a labour market and that it acts like any other commodity market. It is made up of autonomous actors pursuing their own interests and it is governed by supply and demand. But economic anthropologists and those in adjacent disciplines know that it does not always work out that way, that the impersonal market can be more a tale that we tell ourselves than a reality we confront. That taxi driver was learning it, as his addressing that market with his advertising produced little result. Julia Elyachar (2005) describes a different set of people who were learning the same lesson.

They were in el-Hirafiyeen, a suburb of Cairo recently built to house people displaced by new building in the centre of the city. A number of young people in the suburb had enrolled in a scheme sponsored by the US government, training them to be small-scale entrepreneurs. Trainees were taught an economistic view of things: keep careful accounts, pay attention to profit and loss, locate and appeal to the market for what you are selling. They complained to Elyachar: they did not know what this market was or how to find it. Would having a website help? They generated little trade and failed. Like that Port Antonio taxi driver, they should, Elyachar argues, have thought less in terms of markets and more in terms of establishing social relations.

They did not need real friends; only people who knew them and liked them well enough to direct business their way. One way to do this is to see and be seen. People in different places do this in different ways, but most of them revolve around consumption: being sociable over a cup of coffee or a glass of beer or a bottle of soft drink.

It is wrong to think that this sort of sociability is important economically only in peripheral places such as Port Antonio and el-Hirafiyeen; it is important as well in the heartlands of Western economies. Further, it is wrong to think that it is based on the trust that people develop as they deal with each other over an extended period – what I described when I was presenting the difference between gifts and commodities. Rather, this sort of sociality is what Mark Granovetter calls "weak ties".

He says that these are relationships to which the parties devote little time. They have little emotional intensity and are not intimate and they involve few reciprocal services. In other words, people in such relationships are friendly, but not friends. However bland these relationships may seem, they can be important for passing information that is economically important. Granovetter shows this with a study that he did of technical, professional and managerial workers who had recently changed jobs. Such people were more likely to find out about vacancies through personal contact than any other way, and he found that his research subjects learned about the vacancy that became their new job overwhelmingly through weak ties. In over a quarter of cases they got the information from people they saw less than once a year and in over half the cases it was through people they saw more often than that but less than twice a week (Granovetter 1973: 1371).

Granovetter is not the only one to say that the labour market rests more on personal contacts than we might think, but he is unusual for showing that this is true for those in jobs well above the working class, the site of most research on the question. These contacts can be based on many things. For the sort of friendly relationships that concern him, however, they are likely to be based in large part on shared consumption.

In this way the three broad topics in economic anthropology are not a simple chain. Viewed in the abstract, production may lead to the circulation of what is produced and ultimately to its consumption. From the perspective of many of the people involved, however, they form a circle, consumption being a way that people gain access to production.

Becoming consumers

I have described some of the questions that economic anthropologists ask when they study consumption. From what I have said, it is clear that they do not see consumption in the ordinary way, as using something up – what happens when I consume food or my car consumes fuel. In the balance of this chapter I want to lay out one of the important underpinnings of the anthropological view of consumption.

Economic anthropologists, remember, reject the common economists' view that consumption is the individual acquisition of use value, the solitary wolfing down of food. Rather, as I have said repeatedly, it occurs in a social context. We consume in relationships with others, either in the flesh or in our mind's eye. This is easier when the things that we consume are familiar to us. We want to have a sense of where they come from, how they are produced, who is involved, and so on.

This helps account for why the firms that sell flour and chocolate, bananas and other foods in the United States started to put information on their wares that would allow purchasers to go on to a website and see who grew or made them. One wheat farmer, who sells to a milling company that allows purchasers to identify the farm that grew the wheat in the bag of flour that they buy, put it this way: "The person who puts that scone in their mouth can now say, 'Oh my God, there's a real person behind this.' ... They are going to bite into that bread or pastry and know whose hands were on the product" (Stone & Richtel 2009).

In earlier chapters I described historical changes in production and consumption, and Daniel Miller (1987) has analysed those changes and the desire for familiarity at length. In the process, he invokes a definition of "mass consumption" different from "having a lot of stuff". For him, the emergence of mass consumption in Western societies is the emergence of the consumer, by which he means the person who chooses from a variety of objects on offer, in the manner of the economist's market actor.

Miller says that those changes in production and circulation have had two important consequences. The first, arising especially from changes in production, is that people found it harder and harder to express themselves in what they make and to identify themselves with it. The English family that wove cloth stamped themselves on what they made; the worker on the line at Highland Park would find it almost impossible to do so.

The second consequence is that those changes made the things in people's lives less familiar, more impersonal and mysterious. That is because people were less and less likely to know how things are made and more and more likely to acquire them in impersonal transactions. If, then, people want objects to be meaningful socially, they have to provide that meaning themselves. One way that they do so, he says, is through becoming consumers in his sense – people who work at selecting between the objects that they confront – and I have described how Christmas shopping is a heightened instance of this work.

Another way that what people buy can acquire social meaning is through changes in what is in the stores. One aspect of this is something that I have mentioned already: the spread of pre-packaged goods carrying a brand name, which began in earnest in the last quarter of the nineteenth century in the United States and the United Kingdom. As I indicated in an earlier chapter, there is a commercial logic to brands. That is because they help manufacturers to turn an indifferent commodity into something with a distinctive identity, even a personality: not tomato soup or baked beans, but Campbell's soup and Heinz beans. These identities will carry public meanings, but advertising often presents the companies that produce the soup and the beans as social beings, and so helps shoppers to see social meaning in what they are buying.

Changes in store displays in the second half of the nineteenth century, especially in the department stores that were then appearing in big cities, also encouraged people to see things for sale in terms of personal meaning. Conventionally, people who wanted to buy something would have seen items displayed primarily in terms of their utility and cost. For instance, a display of kitchen equipment might have been simply a variety of different pots of different shapes and sizes and prices. In at least some department stores, the new style of display might well have looked like part of a kitchen where someone would be preparing a meal, with perhaps only one or two pots on a counter, as well as knives, bowls and the rest. Such displays were intended to be luxurious and so invoked a range of public meanings, and it is appropriate that around this time shopping was becoming a leisure activity for the richer elements of society. In addition, however, those displays encouraged shoppers to imagine themselves in the kitchen using those pots and other items on display. In doing so, they helped shoppers to locate the items in significant social relations, such as the family or guests for whom they would be preparing a meal.

I have described some changes in commercial practice that encouraged people to be consumers in Miller's sense, selecting items and giving them meaning, and so bring about societies of mass consumption. Other changes obliged people to be consumers in this way.

One thing that obliged them is that household members were less and less likely to work to make things for themselves but, instead, worked to get the money that would enable them to buy things. As I described in an earlier chapter, production moved out of the household and into the factory. This shift from making things in the household to working for pay is not just a consequence of industrialization in the eighteenth and nineteenth centuries. Rather, though for different reasons, it continues into the present.

In the United States, for instance, real wages for hourly workers began to decline early in the 1970s and did not recover for a long time. For production and non-supervisory employees, it took until 2020 for their average hourly earnings to get back to where they had been in 1973 (Federal Reserve Bank of St Louis n.d.). Faced with declining real incomes, many households responded by working more hours, often in the form of having another household member take a job or by having working members take second jobs. This reduced the time available for household work, so that people had to buy more of what they previously made or did for themselves.

Additionally, growing inequality of income has been accompanied by increasing fascination with the lifestyles of the rich and famous, which has raised at least some people's expectations of what a satisfactory level of consumption is. The third-wave coffee at the appropriate shop replaces the older coffee shop; the fancy coffee-making machine at home replaces the older percolator. Similarly, because household members feel pressed for time and because they want something nice, people buy more meals that are prepared and need only to be taken home and heated, or they get something from a takeaway. And if they are really pressed for time they may even have a firm such as Uber Eats deliver it, at a cost that ends up being significantly more than going to the shop and getting it themselves (Chen 2020), much less making it at home.

So it is that the combination of steady or declining income and rising expectations over the past 50 years or so have continued what industrialization started: making many households feel as if they are pressed for money, and so working longer. This means even less time for the household to produce for itself, leading to a greater tendency to buy what they consume, a greater need for money, and so on. Householders become more intensive consumers and mass consumption becomes even more massive.

Afterword

In these chapters I have presented an introduction to economic anthropology. As I said at the outset, I have not tried to be comprehensive. Instead, I have selected and organized ideas and examples in order to illustrate the sorts of things that many economic anthropologists do.

I want to close with a general observation about that doing.

One aspect of the doing is producing detailed descriptions of particular sets of people at particular times, such as the Ponam Islanders that Achsah Carrier and I studied over the course of seven years. Ponams are likely to appear exotic to those who have read this book, but the detailed descriptions can be of people who work in Wall Street investment banks or even a single household in north London. Such descriptions are called ethnography, which A. R. Radcliffe-Brown said is one of the legs on which anthropology stands, and they have long been the staple of anthropological writing.

One could, if one wished, approach that writing for the detailed information that it contains. So, if one liked, one could read all the ethnography of, say, the Melpa, to learn about them and their society.

One could, however, approach the ethnography differently, more in terms of what Radcliffe-Brown called comparative sociology. One could see it as presenting a set of examples of what different sets of people do in their social lives and the factors and processes that seem to shape that doing. Read this way, ethnographies provide evidence of a range of social practices, beliefs and the rest.

These are revealed not by reading everything about the Melpa but by reading ethnography of people anywhere, provided that it describes, for example, the relationship between leadership, an aspect of political organization, and circulation, an aspect of economic practice. Doing this would help us to understand how different sorts of that organization are related to different sorts of that practice. I have tried to indicate this approach from time to time by using processes and practices described for people in distant places and times, and showing how they resemble or differ from what people are doing here and now, and so help make sense of things.

The goal of this is to encourage us to think not about this or that set of people but about various aspects of social life, about how they are different in different places, and why.

Further reading

This presents suggestions for those interested in reading further in and about economic anthropology, ranging from classic texts to journals that regularly publish articles that use economic anthropology.

Classics

These texts have appeared in various editions. For those originally published in English, information on the original edition is listed. Subsequent editions of these works are not materially different.

C. A. Gregory, *Gifts and Commodities* (London: Academic Press, 1982) Gregory taught and did research in Papua New Guinea, which is the book's ethnographic focus, but it ranges much more broadly. The work is a sustained consideration of the different ways that people value things and how they circulate. This is presented in terms of a comparison between the economic principles of neoclassical economics and the practices and values common in Papua New Guinea.

Karl Marx & Friedrich Engels [1848], Part I of *Manifesto of the Communist Party*. Translated by S. Moore (originally published in German) (New York: International Publishers, 1948). Numerous editions. As the title indicates, this is a political manifesto, not a detailed analysis. Part I lays out the basic Marxian view of economic and political organization, asserting the primacy of production and the importance of different classes: sets of people standing in different relations to production and to each other. Although this is not economic anthropology, it has influenced many in the subdiscipline.

Marcel Mauss [1925], *The Gift*. Translated by W. D. Halls (originally published in French) (London: Routledge, 1990). Drawing on material from a variety of societies at different times, this is concerned with how different sorts of circulation link people in different ways and obligate them to each other. Mauss presents those societies in a continuum, from what he called archaic societies at one end to Western market economies at the other.

Karl Polanyi, *The Great Transformation: The Political and Economic Origins of Our Times* (New York: Farrar & Rinehart, 1944). Polanyi analyses politics and economy, primarily in England, from late in the eighteenth century to early in the twentieth. The book looks at the ways that economic activity was decreasingly influenced by social relations and values, commonly called the disembedding of economy from society. It says that this disembedding was not continuous but, rather, that there is what Polanyi calls a double movement: a wave of disembedding led to efforts to re-embed, which led to more disembedding, and so on.

Marshall Sahlins, *Stone Age Economics* (London: Tavistock Press, 1974). Sahlins was important for generating interest in substantivist economic anthropology, and this book contains a variety of substantivist analyses of aspects of socio-economic life. It is organized more as a collection of essays than as a continuous argument. Like Gregory's book, it rejects the formalist idea of universal human economic thought and activity. It is not based on Sahlins's own research but on other people's ethnography.

What economic anthropologists do

In the Preface I said that this book invokes primarily classic statements of approaches and ideas in economic anthropology. To complement that, here are a number of recent books that are economic anthropology, intended to give a sense of the range of recent interest in the subdiscipline.

Julia Elyachar, *Markets of Dispossession: NGOs, Economic Development, and the State in Cairo* (Durham, NC: Duke University Press, 2005). Elyachar investigates the basic economic orientation contained in what was called the Washington Consensus, which reflected fairly formalist microeconomics and was imposed on many countries under the label "structural adjustment".

Egypt was one such country, and to alleviate the poverty caused by structural adjustment the US government funded projects intended to encourage people to start small businesses. Elyachar describes a set of projects, showing how they failed in their aim and suggesting who in fact benefited from them. She says that they failed largely because they saw economic activity as a separate market realm rather than enmeshed in a set of complex social relationships and values, of the sort that the Washington Consensus and neoclassical economics denied.

Karen Ho, *Liquidated: An Ethnography of Wall Street* (Durham, NC: Duke University Press, 2009). The front office of investment banks is the part that creates deals and tries to sell them to investors, and Ho describes them in the context of their practices and economic background. The book describes how banks recruit people to the front office and the mindset those people acquire. It then describes the rise of the idea of shareholder value: that shareholders are the owners of companies and that the companies' main job is to enrich shareholders. This is followed by a description of banks' staffing practices and how they shape the ways that those in the front office see their work and themselves. It ends by indicating that those in the banks took seriously aspects of the image of themselves and the world that they presented, and how this could lead to unfortunate commercial decisions.

Deborah James, *Money from Nothing: Indebtedness and Aspiration in South Africa* (Stanford, CA: Stanford University Press, 2015). Financial inclusion means encouraging people to tap into financial markets by borrowing money, having web-based accounts and the like. South Africa sought to increase financial inclusion, and this book describes the practical operation and consequences for people's lives. Many embraced finance, thinking that it would help them to achieve membership in the middle class. The consequence was high levels of debt, and the book describes forms of advice about debt and support for debtors, ranging from networks of kin and neighbours through formal debt counselling to charismatic churches.

Massimiliano Mollona, *Made in Sheffield: An Ethnography of Industrial Work and Politics* (Oxford: Berghahn, 2009). Sheffield is a site of declining steel making in Britain, and Mollona studied metalworkers there. He is concerned with two types of workers: skilled artisans, who have a fair amount of control over their work; and those who work in one of the remaining large steel plants, with little control. Large plants try to survive by working their labour harder. The smaller artisanal firms survive by turning themselves into what are effectively patriarchal, peasant household enterprises that engage in some activities aimed at the market and some not. Mollona relates work in these two different situations to other areas of workers' lives, especially household organization and urban politics.

Andrea Muehlebach, *The Moral Neoliberal: Welfare and Citizenship in Italy* (Chicago, IL: University of Chicago Press, 2012). This book focuses on the area around Milan as people and organizations responded to the withdrawal of state services and support usually seen as an expression of neoliberal ideology. It describes how that response included a marked expansion of charitable and related work to improve people's lives, resting on ideas from a variety of groups, especially the Catholic Church. The state services were offered to all as a matter of right, whereas the charity was offered to those who were seen to deserve it. As a result, neoliberal reform has led to a change in what it means to be a citizen and the rights that accrue to citizens.

Emil A. Røyrvik, *The Allure of Capitalism* (New York: Berghahn, 2011). Hydro, a large Norwegian company that operates in many parts of the world, is Røyrvik's focus. He is concerned particularly with what management does in the company and how management decision-making practices affect aspects of company activities. One of the important things that the book describes is policies that seek to quantify decision making, using what are called "metrics" to provide what seems to be an objective basis for decisions about things such as where to set up new projects.

Andrew Sanchez, *Criminal Capital: Violence, Corruption and Class in Industrial India* (Abingdon: Routledge, 2016). Sanchez did fieldwork in a large steel firm in India, interested in how it operates and the people who are employed there. The book has two main concerns. One is the changing position of labour, as older patterns of permanent employment give way to short-term work – a change that has been common in industry in India, as in much of the world. It describes management's justifications for this and its effects on workers and their families. The other is corruption, in the sense of both the illegal and the dishonest, which it says reflects, among other things, the state's failure to investigate and punish it. The book argues that corruption is a necessary part of large-scale commerce in India and, arguably, many part of the world.

Gillian Tett, *Fool's Gold: How Unrestrained Greed Corrupted a Dream, Shattered Global Markets and Unleashed a Catastrophe* (London: Abacus, 2009). Tett was trained as an anthropologist, and she ended up in a senior editorial position at the *Financial Times*. Her book describes the development of complex financial instruments of the sort that led to the financial crisis of 2008. That began with the development of sophisticated formulae and computation techniques, which became widespread in the financial sector and were adopted by a set of financial traders, who resisted attempts to regulate or even investigate the trades that they were making and the models that led them to make them.

Caitlin Zaloom, *Out of the Pits: Traders and Technology from Chicago to London* (Chicago, IL: University of Chicago Press, 2006). In the trade of financial derivatives, traders seek to profit not by buying things such as pork bellies or German government bonds but by buying and selling the opportunity to buy them. One main concern of Zaloom's book is the ways that traders operate in two different environments. One is the trading floor, where traders are in each other's presence and shout their orders to each other. The other is electronic, with traders sitting in front of computers, looking at prices and trading accordingly. She argues that the electronic trading relies on software and systems that treat trading activity as an impersonal market, which is different from the more social and complex interactions that are important on the trading floor.

Topics and concepts in economic anthropology

There are sources that describe specific concepts in economic anthropology and areas of interest to economic anthropologists. First, however, there is a book by an important economic anthropologist that lays out his understanding of the field.

Richard Wilk, *Economies and Cultures: Foundations of Economic Anthropology* (Boulder, CO: Westview Press, 1996).

I provide three sources for those interested in concepts and areas of interest. The table of contents of each will suggest entries of interest to readers, and I also indicate some of the more pertinent entries.

Hilary Callan (ed.), *International Encyclopedia of Anthropology* (Oxford: Wiley-Blackwell, 2018). The material on economic anthropology was organized by Chris Hann. Web address for economic anthropology entries: https://onlinelibrary.wiley.com/browse/book/10.1002/9781118924396/topic? ConceptID=216029&seriesKey=mrwseries&tagCode=.

Pertinent entries: Alienation. Capitalism. Commodity. Consumption. Credit and debt. Economic anthropology. Economy, cultural approaches to. Economy, feminist approaches to. Finance. Gender and economics. Gift. Household. Industrial workers. Kula. Labor, employment, and work. Markets. Polanyi, Karl. Property. Shopping. Work.

James G. Carrier (ed.), *A Handbook of Economic Anthropology*, second edition (Cheltenham: Edward Elgar, 2012). Web address: www.e-elgar. com/shop/usd/a-handbook-of-economic-anthropology-second-edition-9781781004494.html.

Pertinent entries: Anthropology – of the financial crisis. Community and economy. Consumption. Economic crisis, 2008. The gift and gift economy. Property. Provisioning.

James G. Carrier (ed.), *A Research Agenda for Economic Anthropology* (Cheltenham: Edward Elgar, 2019). This volume is organized differently from the preceding, but has chapters that consider specific topics. *Web address*: www.e-elgar.com/shop/gbp/a-research-agenda-for-economic-anthropology-9781788116091.html.

Pertinent entries: Debt, financialisation and politics. Inequality. Resources: Nature, value and time.

Journals

Articles that count as economic anthropology appear from time to time in just about all anthropology journals. There are four that are more likely to have material related to economic anthropology, however.

Economic Anthropology (https://anthrosource.onlinelibrary.wiley.com/journal/23304847).

Focaal (www.berghahnjournals.com/view/journals/focaal/focaal-overview. xml). Issue 87 (June 2020) has a set of articles on financialization and debt.

PoLAR [*Political and Legal Anthropology Review*] (https://anthrosource. onlinelibrary.wiley.com/journal/15552934).

Research in Economic Anthropology (www.emerald.com/insight/publication/issn/0190-1281). This appears as an annual issue.

References

NB: articles in *The New York Times* can be located by searching for the article title on their website, www.nytimes.com.

Abelson, R. 2019. "Hospitals sue Trump to keep negotiated prices secret". *New York Times*, 4 December.

Archer, M. & J. Blau 1993. "Class formation in nineteenth-century America: the case of the middle class". *Annual Review of Sociology* 19: 17–41. www.jstor.org/stable/2083379.

Arrighi, G. 1994. *The Long Twentieth Century: Money, Power and the Origins of Our Times*. London: Verso.

Barnett, S. & M. Silverman 1979. "Separations in capitalist societies: persons, things, units and relations". In *Ideology and Everyday Life*, S. Barnett & M. Silverman (eds), 39–81. Ann Arbor, MI: University of Michigan Press.

Baudrillard, J. 1981 [1968]. *For a Critique of the Political Economy of the Sign*, C. Levin (trans.). St Louis, MO: Telos Press.

Belk, R. 1993. "Materialism and the making of the modern American Christmas". In *Unwrapping Christmas*, D. Miller (ed.), 75–104. Oxford: Clarendon Press.

Berle, A. & G. Means 1932. *The Modern Corporation and Private Property*. New York: Harcourt, Brace, World.

Bilton, N. 2014. "Steve Jobs was a low-tech parent". *New York Times*, 10 September.

Blaug, M. 2003. "The Formalist revolution of the 1950s." In *A Companion to the History of Economic Thought*, W. Samuels, J. Biddle & J. Davis (eds), 395–410. Malden, MA: Blackwell.

Borsay, P. 1989. *The English Urban Renaissance: Culture and Society in the Provincial Town, 1660–1770*. Oxford: Clarendon Press.

Bourdieu, P. 1977 [1972]. *Outline of a Theory of Practice*, R. Nice (trans.). Cambridge: Cambridge University Press.

Bourdieu, P. 1984 [1979]. *Distinction: A Social Critique of the Judgement of Taste*, R. Nice (trans.). London: Routledge & Kegan Paul.

Boylan, J. 2019. "My very marry Christmas. Why do we love getting engaged around the holidays?". *New York Times*, 25 December.

Braverman, H. 1974. *Labor and Monopoly Capital: The Degradation of Work in the Twentieth Century*. New York: Monthly Review Press.

Brunton, R. 1975. "Why do the Trobriands have chiefs?" *Man* 10 (4): 544–58. DOI: 10.2307/2800132.

Burawoy, M. 1982. *Manufacturing Consent: Changes in the Labor Process under Monopoly Capitalism*. Chicago, IL: University of Chicago Press.

Burke, K. 1969. *A Grammar of Motives*. Berkeley, CA: University of California Press.

Burrough, B. & J. Helyar 1990. *Barbarians at the Gate: The Fall of RJR Nabisco*. New York: Harper & Row.

Caplow, T. 1984. "Rule enforcement without visible means: Christmas gift giving in Middletown". *American Journal of Sociology* 89 (6): 1306–23. DOI: 10.1086/228017.

Carrier, A. & J. Carrier 1991. *Structure and Process in a Melanesian Society: Ponam's Progress in the Twentieth Century*. London: Harwood Academic.

Carrier, J. 1992. "Emerging alienation in production: a Maussian history". *Man* 27 (3): 539–58. DOI: 10.2307/2803928.

Carrier, J. 2018a. "Commodity". In *The International Encyclopedia of Anthropology*, H. Callan (ed.), 1015–22. Oxford: Wiley-Blackwell.

Carrier, J. 2018b. "Moral economy: what's in a name?". *Anthropological Theory* 18 (1): 18–35. DOI: 10.1177/1463499617735259.

Carrier, J. & A. Carrier 1989. *Wage, Trade and Exchange in Melanesia: A Manus Society in the Modern State*. Berkeley, CA: University of California Press.

Carrier, J. & A. Carrier 1990. "Every picture tells a story: visual alternatives to oral tradition in Ponam society". *Oral Tradition* 5 (2/3) [special issue on the South Pacific; R. Finnegan & M. Orbell, eds]: 354–75. https://journal.oraltradition.org/wp-content/uploads/files/articles/5ii-iii/11_carrier_carrier.pdf.

Carson, G. 1954. *The Old Country Store*. New York: Oxford University Press.

Chen, B. 2020. "Up to 91% more expensive: how delivery apps eat up your budget". *New York Times*, 26 February.

Coase, R. 1937. "The nature of the firm". *Economica* 4 (16): 386–405. DOI: 10.1111/j.1468-0335.1937.tb00002.x.

Crowley, J. 1974. *This Sheba, Self: The Conceptualization of Economic Life in Eighteenth-Century America*. Baltimore, MD: Johns Hopkins University Press.

Csikszentmihalyi, M. & E. Rochberg-Halton 1981. *The Meaning of Things: Domestic Symbols and the Self*. New York: Cambridge University Press.

Davidoff, L. & C. Hall 1987. *Family Fortunes: Men and Women of the English Middle Class, 1780–1850*. Chicago, IL: University of Chicago Press.

DealBook 2009. "Blankfein says he's just doing 'God's work'". *New York Times*, 9 November.

Dickens, C. 1918 [1843]. *A Christmas Carol*. Philadelphia, PA: Henry Altemus Co.

Donner, H. 2015. "Making middle-class families in Calcutta". In *Anthropologies of Class: Power, Practice and Inequality*, J. Carrier & D. Kalb (eds), 131–48. Cambridge: Cambridge University Press.

Dore, R. 1983. "Goodwill and the spirit of market capitalism". *British Journal of Sociology* 34 (4): 459–82. DOI: 10.2307/590932.

Douglas, M. 1966. *Purity and Danger*. London: Routledge & Kegan Paul.

Douglas, M. & B. Isherwood 1978. *The World of Goods: Towards an Anthropology of Consumption*. Harmondsworth: Penguin Books.

Elyachar, J. 2005. *Markets of Dispossession: NGOs, Economic Development, and the State in Cairo*. Durham, NC: Duke University Press.

Emerson, R. 1983 [1844]. "Gifts". In *The Collected Works of Ralph Waldo Emerson*, vol. 3, *Essays: Second Series*, A. Ferguson & J. Carr (eds), 91–6. Cambridge, MA: Harvard University Press. Available at: https://emersoncentral.com/texts/essays-second-series/gifts.

Everitt, A. 1967. "The marketing of agricultural produce". In *The Agrarian History of England and Wales*, vol. 4, *1500–1640*, J. Thirsk (ed.), 466–592. Cambridge: Cambridge University Press.

Federal Reserve Bank of St Louis n.d. "Average hourly earnings of production and nonsupervisory employees, total private/consumer price index for all urban consumers: all items in U.S. city average". St Louis: Economic Research, Federal Reserve Bank of St Louis. https://fred.stlouisfed.org/graph/?g=u8sg.

Fischer, E. 2020. "Quality and inequality: creating value worlds with third wave coffee". *Socio-Economic Review* (in press). DOI: 10.1093/ser/mwz044.

Frank, A. 1966. "The development of underdevelopment". *Monthly Review* 18 (4): 17–30. DOI: 10.14452/MR-018-04-1966-08_3.

Friedman, J. 2002a. "Champagne liberals and the new 'dangerous classes': reconfigurations of class, identity and cultural production in the contemporary global system". *Social Analysis* 46 (2): 33–55. www.jstor.org/stable/23170150.

Friedman, J. 2002b. "From roots to routes: tropes for trippers". *Anthropological Theory* 2 (1): 21–36. DOI: 10.1177/1463499602002001286.

Friedman, J. 2013. "Globalization in anthropology". In *The Handbook of Sociocultural Anthropology*, J. Carrier & D. Gewertz (eds), 355–69. London: Bloomsbury.

Frost, K. 2018. "The most popular day for marriage proposals is still to come". *Harper's Bazaar*, 11 December. www.harpersbazaar.com/uk/bazaar-brides/a13769120/most-popular-day-for-marriage-proposals.

Golby, J. 1981. "A history of Christmas". In *Popular Culture: Themes and Issues*, vol. 1, T. Bennett (ed.), 8–26. Milton Keynes: Open University Press.

Granovetter, M. 1973. "The strength of weak ties". *American Journal of Sociology* 78 (6): 1360–80. DOI: 10.1086/225469.

Granovetter, M. 1985. "Economic action and social structure: the problem of embeddedness". *American Journal of Sociology* 91 (3): 481–510. www.jstor.org/stable/2780199.

Gregory, C. 1980. "Gifts to men and gifts to God: gift exchange and capital accumulation in contemporary Papua". *Man* 15 (4): 626–52. DOI: 10.2307/2801537.

Gregory, C. 1982. *Gifts and Commodities*. London: Academic Press.

Grieco, M. 1987. *Keeping It in the Family: Social Networks and Employment Chance*. London: Tavistock Press.

Gudeman, S. & A. Rivera 1991. *Conversations in Colombia: The Domestic Economy in Life and Text*. New York: Cambridge University Press.

Halle, D. 1984. *America's Working Man: Work, Home, and Politics among Blue-Collar Property Owners*. Chicago, IL: University of Chicago Press.

Henry, O. 1917 [1905]. "The gift of the magi". In *The Four Million*, 16–25. New York: Doubleday, Page.

Hirsch, E. 1992. "The long term and the short term of domestic consumption: an ethnographic case study". In *Consuming Technologies: Media and Information in Domestic Spaces*, R. Silverstone & E. Hirsch (eds), 208–26. London: Routledge.

Ho, K. 2009. *Liquidated: An Ethnography of Wall Street*. Durham, NC: Duke University Press.

Ho, K. 2012. "Finance". In *A Companion to Moral Anthropology*, D. Fassin (ed.), 413–31. Malden, MA: Wiley-Blackwell.

Hochschild, A. 1983. *The Managed Heart: The Commercialization of Human Feeling*. Berkeley, CA: University of California Press.

Hounshell, D. 1984. *From the American System to Mass Production, 1800–1932*. Baltimore, MD: Johns Hopkins University Press.

Irving, W. 1809. *A History of New York from the Beginning of the World to the End of the Dutch Dynasty, by Diedrich Knickerbocker* [commonly called *Knickerbocker's History*]. New York: Inskeep & Bradford.

Jones, C. 1978. *Saint Nicholas of Myra, Bari, and Manhattan*. Chicago, IL: University of Chicago Press.

Jones, G. 1971. *Outcast London: A Study in the Relationship between Classes in Victorian Society*. Oxford: Clarendon Press.

Jones, O. 2011. *Chavs: The Demonization of the Working Class*. London: Verso.

Kondo, M. 2014. *The Life-Changing Magic of Tidying Up: The Japanese Art of Decluttering and Organizing*. New York: Ten Speed Press.

Krugman, P. 2019. "Trump hits the panic button". *New York Times*, 12 September.

Lehrer, T. 1959. "A Christmas carol". In *An Evening Wasted with Tom Lehrer*. Lehrer Records. www.youtube.com/watch?v=DtZR3lJobjw.

Lévi-Strauss, C. 1969 [1962]. *Totemism*, R. Needham (trans.). Harmondsworth: Penguin Books.

McKendrick, N., J. Brewer & J. Plumb 1982. *The Birth of a Consumer Society: The Commercialization of Eighteenth-Century England*. Bloomington, IN: Indiana University Press.

Malinowski, B. 1922. *Argonauts of the Western Pacific*. London: Routledge.

Marx, K. & F. Engels 1948 [1848]. *Manifesto of the Communist Party*, S. Moore (trans.). New York: International Publishers.

Mathias, P. 1967. *Retailing Revolution: A History of Multiple Retailing in the Food Trades based upon the Allied Suppliers Group of Companies*. London: Longman.

Mauss, M. 1990 [1925]. *The Gift: The Form and Reason for Exchange in Archaic Societies*, W. Halls (trans.). London: Routledge.

Mayhew, H. 1849. "Letter XVII." *Morning Chronicle*, 14 December. Available at: www.victorianlondon.org/mayhew/mayhew17.htm.

Miller, D. 1987. *Material Culture and Mass Consumption*. Oxford: Basil Blackwell.

Miller, D. 1988. "Appropriating the state on the council estate". *Man* 23 (2): 353–72. DOI: 10.2307/2802810.

Miller, D. 1994. *Modernity: An Ethnographic Approach*. Oxford: Berg.

Miller, D. 1998. *A Theory of Shopping*. Cambridge: Polity Press.

Mintz, S. 1985. *Sweetness and Power: The Place of Sugar in Modern History*. New York: Viking.

Mui, H.-C. & L. Mui 1989. *Shops and Shopkeeping in Eighteenth Century England*. London: Routledge.

Muppets 1992. *The Muppet Christmas Carol*. Burbank, CA: Disney Pictures, Jim Henson Productions.

Parry, J. 1986. "*The Gift*, the Indian gift and the 'Indian Gift' ". *Man* 21 (3): 453–73. DOI: 10.2307/2803096.

Parsons, T. 1959. "The social structure of the family". In *The Family: Its Function and Destiny*, R. Anshen (ed.), 241–74. New York: Harper & Row.

Pennington, S. & B. Westover 1989. *A Hidden Workforce: Homeworkers in England, 1850–1985*. Basingstoke: Macmillan.

Pimlott, J. 1978. *The Englishman's Christmas: A Social History*. Brighton: Harvester Press.

Polanyi, K. 1944. *The Great Transformation: The Political and Economic Origins of Our Time*. New York: Farrar & Rinehart.

Polanyi, K. 1957. "The economy as instituted process". In *Trade and Market in the Early Empires: Economies in History and Theory*, K. Polanyi, C. Arensberg & H. Pearson (eds), 243–70. Glencoe, IL: Free Press.

Polson, M. 2018. "Marketing marijuana: prohibition, medicalization and the commodity". In *Economy, Crime and Wrong in a Neoliberal Era*, J. Carrier (ed.), 140–71. Oxford: Berghahn.

Price, R. 1966. "Caribbean fishing and fishermen: a historical sketch". *American Anthropologist* 68 (6): 1364–83. www.jstor.org/stable/670650.

Radcliffe-Brown, A. 1952. *Structure and Function in Primitive Society*. London: Routledge & Kegan Paul.

Raspberry, W. 1988. "Christmas run amok: our gift-giving has gotten out of hand". *Washington Post*, 4 January.

Reilly, K. 2016. "Read Hillary Clinton's 'basket of deplorables' remark about Donald Trump supporters". *Time*, 10 September. http://time.com/4486502/hillary-clinton-basket-of-deplorables-transcript.

Rivzi, S. 2003. "Postwar neoclassical microeconomics". In *A Companion to the History of Economic Thought*, W. Samuels, J. Biddle & J. Davis (eds), 377–94. Malden, MA: Blackwell.

Robbins, L. 1945 [1932]. *An Essay on the Nature and Significance of Economic Science*. London: Macmillan.

Sahlins, M. 1963. "Poor man, rich man, big-man, chief: political types in Melanesia and Polynesia". *Comparative Studies in Society and History* 5 (3): 285–303. www.jstor.org/stable/177650.

Sahlins, M. 1974. *Stone Age Economics*. London: Tavistock Press.

Santos, F. 2019. "Who will wear my dead husband's clothes? It took me a long time to find a new home for the belongings he left behind". *New York Times*, 1 November.

Schneider, D. 1980. *American Kinship: A Cultural Account*, 2nd edn. Chicago, IL: University of Chicago Press.

Scott, J. 1976. *The Moral Economy of the Peasant: Rebellion and Subsistence in Southeast Asia*. New Haven, CT: Yale University Press.

Shames, L. 1986. *The Big Time: Harvard Business School's Most Successful Class – and How it Shaped America*. New York: Harper Collins.

Silver, A. 1990. "Friendship in commercial society: eighteenth-century social theory and modern sociology". *American Journal of Sociology* 95 (6): 1474–504. DOI: 10.1086/229461.

Smelser, N. 1959. *Social Change in the Industrial Revolution: An Application of Theory to the British Cotton Industry*. Chicago, IL: University of Chicago Press.

Smith, A. 1976 [1776]. *An Inquiry into the Nature and Causes of the Wealth of Nations*. Chicago, IL: University of Chicago Press.

Smith, A. 1984 [1759]. *The Theory of Moral Sentiments*. Indianapolis, IN: Liberty Fund.

Staples, W. 1987. "Technology, control, and the social organization of work at a British hardware firm, 1791–1891". *American Journal of Sociology* 93 (1): 62–88. www.jstor.org/stable/2779673.

Stewart, J. 2017. "Barclays's latest problem: questions on chief's judgment". *New York Times*, 11 May.

Stone, B. & M. Richtel 2009. "Forging a hot link to the farmer who grows the food". *New York Times*, 27 March.

Strasser, S. 1989. *Satisfaction Guaranteed: The Making of the American Mass Market*. New York: Pantheon.

Strathern, A. 1971. *The Rope of Moka: Big-Men and Ceremonial Exchange in Mount Hagen, New Guinea*. Cambridge: Cambridge University Press.

Tankersley, J., P. Eavis & B. Casselman 2019. "How FedEx cut its tax bill to $0". *New York Times*, 17 November.

Taylor, F. 1919 [1911]. *The Principles of Scientific Management*. New York: Harper & Brothers.

Thompson, E. 1967. "Time, work discipline and industrial capitalism". *Past & Present* 38: 56–98. DOI: 10.1093/past/38.1.56.

Thompson, E. 1968. *The Making of the English Working Class*. Harmondsworth: Penguin Books.

Thompson, E. 1971. "The moral economy of the English crowd in the eighteenth century". *Past & Present* 50: 76–136. www.jstor.org/stable/650244.

Tolkien, J. 1937. *The Hobbit*. London: Allen & Unwin.

Tversky, A. & D. Kahneman 1974. "Judgment under uncertainty: heuristics and biases". *Science* 185: 1124–31. DOI: 10.1126/science.185.4157.1124.

Twentieth Century Fox 1947. *Miracle on 34th Street*. Los Angeles: Twentieth Century Fox.

Universal Pictures 2003. *Love Actually*. Universal City, CA: Universal Pictures.

Veblen, T. 1927 [1899]. *The Theory of the Leisure Class*. New York: Vanguard Press.

Wallerstein, I. 1974. *The Modern World-System*, vol. 1, *Capitalist Agriculture and the Origins of the European World-Economy in the Sixteenth Century*. New York: Academic Press.

Walsh, W. 1986. *The Rise and Decline of the Great Atlantic & Pacific Tea Company*. Secaucus, NJ: Lyle Stuart.

Wilk, R. 1994. "'I hate pizza': distaste and dislike in the consuming lives of Belizeans". Paper presented at the annual meeting of the American Anthropological Association, Atlanta, 30 November.

Wilk, R. 1996. *Economies and Cultures: Foundations of Economic Anthropology*. Boulder, CO: Westview Press.

Williamson, O. 1975. *Markets and Hierarchies, Analysis and Antitrust Implications: A Study in the Economics of Internal Organization*. New York: Free Press.

Wilson, P. 1973. *Crab Antics: The Social Anthropology of English-Speaking Negro Societies of the Caribbean*. New Haven, CT: Yale University Press.

Woolworth, F. 1954. *Woolworth's First 75 Years*. New York: F. W. Woolworth.

Work, H. 1864. "Come home, father". Chicago, IL: Root & Cady.

Yuan, L. 2019. "How Huawei lost the heart of the Chinese public". *New York Times*, 4 December.

Zimmerman, M. 1937. *Super Market: Spectacular Exponent of Mass Distribution.* New York: Super Market Publishing.

Index